The Best of Forgotten English

Published by Sellers Publishing, Inc.

161 John Roberts Road, South Portland, Maine 04106
www.sellerspublishing.com • E-mail: rsp@rsvp.com

Production by Charlotte Cromwell

ISBN 13: 978-1-4162-4599-5
Library of Congress Control Number: 2016930767

10 9 8 7 6 5 4 3 2 1

Printed in the United States of America.

The Best of
Forgotten English

Vanishing Vocabulary
and *Folklore*

Jeff Kacirk

SELLERS

PUBLISHING

Contents

Introduction

The development of the English language has certainly provided writers with plenty of subject matter. My love of lost examples of earlier English — some dating back well into medieval times — is hopelessly entangled with my fascination regarding social history, and the goal of my writing has been to try to bring these two worlds together. In hunting for former expressions, curious tidbits and outdated social customs, my journey has unexpectedly taken me down many rabbit holes and into the linguistic shrubbery.

My research turned up enough castoff words and remarkable stories to weave together vignettes of the past, week in and week out, for twenty years. While working, I often begin by asking myself specific questions and, as I look for answers, they often broaden into others. Some questions are answered and some not, but seldom do I come away without discovering something new and interesting about the past. Until Victorian times, for example, did most Europeans bathe only once a year — if at all? Were the blades of windmills used to transmit messages? Have animals and inanimate objects, such as ladders and boats, ever been tried for crimes, including murder? Explanations of these and hundreds of other questions are found in these pages.

Over the years, readers have asked for a more permanent edition of *Forgotten English* for their libraries, which I am pleased to finally offer. But what to include in a book version? Many aspects of everyday life have a history, and I considered more than thirty chapter subjects for these pages. Topics that ended up on the cutting room floor ran the gamut from folk tales and architecture to descriptions of far-flung places and military adventures. I chose instead to focus on subjects with ongoing relevance, keeping in mind the words of Jean-Baptiste Karr, who wrote in 1849,

"The more things change, the more they remain the same." So my calendars examine people's occupations, religious practices, courtships, food and drink, artistic expressions and, above all, the ever-changing English language as natural subjects.

These entries contain backstories that explore the lighter side of history, punctuated with thought-provoking darker moments. My favorites include sketches of manners and etiquette, such as how being "fashionably late" began, the advent of men's fashion accessory called a codpiece, and the use of a diner's thumbnail to spread butter. Puzzling medical beliefs and mistakes are also presented, including the 18th-century use of tar-water as a cure-all, strange dieting regimens and Benjamin Franklin's odd remedy for flatulence. Misbehavior among aristocrats, attorneys, politicians, royalty, and the clergy has not gone unnoticed, nor have curious ideas and inventions. The evolution of questionable practices and devices into modern ones — such as prison hardware called the treadmill — are found here too.

Samples of early English occupy a special place at the top of each entry because they are especially important to me. So in the book's final chapter I am pleased to offer 200 additional relics from earlier times — a "lumping pennyworth," as residents of Essex, England once called a generous spoonful of spices. This small collection of linguistic fossils is intended to further pique interest in "archaic" terms — most of which were simply abandoned or replaced when more useful ones came along. With the benefit of hindsight, my sense is that combining these discarded words and phrases with historical texts and stories, softened with a little humor, makes the reading experience a more rounded and valuable one. To my long-time readers, thank you for your support, comments and kind corrections over the years, and to everyone else, welcome.

The Dynamic English Language

There is no basis for the belief that somewhere there exists a sublimated English language, perfect and impeccable. Nowhere is this speech without stain spoken by man in his daily life — not in London, where cockneyisms abound, not in Oxford, where university slang is luxuriant and where pedantry flourishes. Nowhere has this pure and undefiled language ever been spoken by any community. Nowhere will it ever be spoken, other than by a few men here and there gifted by nature or trained by art.

—American author James Brander Matthews's
Americanisms and Briticisms, 1892

duopoly

A condition in which there are only two suppliers of a certain commodity, service, etc. The domination of a particular market by two firms. Hence *duopolist*, one member of a duopoly; *duopolize*, to engross between two.

—Sir James Murray's *New English Dictionary*, 1893

Neither Borrower Nor Lender Be

In *Grammatica Linguae Anglicanae* (1685), English grammarian Christopher Cooper condemned the importing of foreign expressions into English: "Our language is so constituted that it is very easy to make new words, or to adapt strange ones, so that there is no art or science which cannot be fully and copiously dealt with in English. But the greatest care ought to be taken [and] the advice of learned grammarians and the authority of magistracy [government] should be sought before new or strange words should be admitted into common use. For this childish (shall I say *mad?*) affectation of words is absolutely blameworthy, when much more suitable ones could be drawn from our own fount. The affected words obscure the native propriety of the language and make the language itself untrue to its own nature, confused, uncertain, and burdened with a useless weight of words."

moonflaw

The wild fancy of a lunatic. *Moonling*, a lunatic.

—Charles Mackay's *Lost Beauties of the English Language*, 1874

An Unsettling Discovery

In 1872, expatriate American medical doctor William Minor (shown here) murdered a London brewery worker, whom he mistakenly believed was stalking him. Minor had been traumatized by Civil War duty a decade earlier and was increasingly burdened by paranoia. For his deed he was committed for life to Broadmoor, a state-of-the-art English lunatic asylum. But due to his financial circumstances Minor was able to afford a double-sized cell, which he furnished with a private library.

Six years later, after reading about the project then under way to compile the *New English Dictionary* (the forerunner of the *Oxford English Dictionary*), he began submitting literary citations to editor James Murray. Eventually, more than 12,000 of Minor's snippets were incorporated into this massive dictionary, which was published in installments between 1888 and 1928. But Minor's condition remained a mystery to Murray during most of their long and cordial postal relationship. Assuming Minor to be a reclusive member of the asylum's staff, Murray eventually visited his pen pal only to learn the startling truth on his arrival.

opiniastrous

Unduly attached to one's own opinion.
—Noah Webster's *American Dictionary of the English Language*, 1828

Spelling in America

Noah Webster (1758-1843) has long been considered among America's most influential lexicographers. He helped Americanize certain English words, differentiating such spellings as *salad* from the traditional *sallet*, *showed* from *shewed*, and *jail* from *gaol*. But Webster also tried unsuccessfully to change, among others, *build* to *bild*, *island* to *ieland*, and the long-used *bridegroom* to *bridegoom*, because it came from Old English *bryd-guma*. Regarding *bridegroom*, he scolded those who opposed his pedantic version, saying, "Such a corruption ought not to remain a blight to philology."

In addition, at least a dozen contemporaries, including Benjamin Franklin, proposed in books, pamphlets, and magazine articles various modifications regarding spelling. These included William Thornton's *Cadmus* (1793) which called on Americans, having "corrected the dangerous doctrines of European powers" to next amend their language, saying, "The American language will thus be

as distinct as the government, free of all the follies of unphilosophical fashion, and resting upon truth as its only regulator." Other ineffective advocates of spelling reform were James Ewing in *Columbian Alphabet* (1798) and William Pelham in *System of Notation* (1808).

grammaticaster

A pedantic, trifling grammarian. From Late Latin *grammaticus.*

—C. A. M. Fennell's *Stanford Dictionary of Anglicised Words and Phrases,* 1892

Haberdasher of nouns, schoolmaster.

—B. E. Gent's *Dictionary of the Termes of the Canting Crew,* c. 1699

Americanisms as Foreign Words

In 1737, Englishman Francis Moore penned in his diary the first written denouncement of an Americanism — a practice carried on by his countrymen for the next two centuries. The offending word, *bluff,* had been adapted by Americans from its traditional but now largely forgotten British meaning of a jutting ship's prow, to also describe a somewhat similarly shaped piece of land atop an embankment. Moore described one view of Savannah, Georgia: "It stands upon the flat of a hill; the bank of the river (which they in barbarous English call a *bluff*) is steep, and about forty-five foot perpendicular."

Long afterward, English lexicographer and grammarian Henry Fowler continued the assault on Americans and their patterns of speech in *The King's English* (1906), writing scornfully, "Everyone knows an Americanism when he sees it," and "Americanisms are foreign words, and should be so treated."

plottage

The area of a plot of land, the deplorable result of an illicit union between *plot* and *acreage*.

—Eric Partridge's *Chamber of Horrors: A Glossary of Official Jargon, Both English and American,* 1952

Usage and Abusage

Eric Honeywood Partridge (1894–1979), noted New Zealand–born lexicographer, delighted in focusing on slang and what he liked to call "word abusage." Along with verbs that have been converted into legitimate-sounding nouns through the application of the suffix –*age*, such as *wreckage, leakage, mileage,* and *passage,* he cited terms that have received artificial prestige from that same appendage, such as *parentage, signage,* and Shakespeare's *baggage.*

But many ludicrous –*age* barbarisms have fallen by the wayside, including *eatage, fruitage, vagabondage,* and *dumpage.* Other obsolete examples include *rivage* (a river bank), *umpirage* (an umpire's power), *waterage* (travel by boat), *concubinage* (a den of ill repute), *imposturage* (an imposter's actions), *lawyerage* (an attorney's

home), *stumpage* (logging rights), *flobbage* (phlegm), *lactage* (dairy products), *scrappage* (food scraps), *muirage* (taxes for building walls), *clownage* (the actions of a clown), and *rattage* (loss by rats). Mercifully we have been spared the likes of *burglage* for burglary, *shrubbage* for shrubbery, and *scenage* for scenery, as well as *wrappage.* But the English still use *haylage* to refer to animal fodder.

bungfunger

To startle; to confuse. Also used as an adjective for confounded. Compare with *bumsquabbled*, defeated, stupified [and] *bum-fiddled*. "I am now *bum-fiddled* with a bastard." John Fletcher's play *The Chances* (1620).

—John Farmer's *Slang and Its Analogues*, 1890–1904

Slang Unleashed

In 1890, the first of seven volumes of John Farmer's comprehensive look at *Slang and Its Analogues* was published. Farmer was born in England but lived much of his life in the United States, yet chose to focus on American English. So his inclusion of expressions ranging from the colorful to the slightly off-color from both sides of the Atlantic is not surprising.

The preface states: "Authorities differ between themselves — and often with themselves — when asked to set down in plain scientific terms the marks which distinguish vagrant words of slang from correct and orthodox English. The borderland between slang and the Queen's English is an ill-defined territory, the limits of which have never been clearly mapped out. It is, therefore, not without hesitation that I have ventured to explore this 'Dark Continent' of the World of Words." But in his earlier *Americanisms, Old and New* (1889) Farmer assured readers, "These words, phrases, and colloquialisms, which at first sight seem novel, uncouth, and obscene are, when scrutinised, found to possess a parentage that cannot be questioned."

auricoation

The act or practice of driving carriages.
—Samuel Johnson's *Dictionary of the English Language*, 1755

Samuel Johnson's Dictionary

Although this celebrated man of letters once admitted, "If I had no duties and no reference to futurity, I would spend my life in driving briskly in a post-chaise with a pretty woman," his most satisfying moments probably came from his writing.

Dr. Johnson's heralded dictionary was the first to use copious literary quotations to illustrate entries. In the preface, he absolved himself from "a few wild blunders and risible absurdities, from which no work of multiplicity was ever free," and mentioned the dynamic nature of the English language — the ongoing process by which it grows and simultaneously sheds words: "No dictionary of a living tongue ever can be perfect, since while it is hastening to production,  some words are budding and some falling away; that a whole life cannot be spent on syntax and etymology, and that even a whole life would not be sufficient." He then dedicated his nine years of efforts to a catching up with England's linguistic rival, the Académie française: "In hope of giving longevity to that which its own nature forbids to be immortal, I have devoted this book, the labour of years, to the honour of my country, that we may no longer yield the palm of philology without a contest to the nations of the continent."

language of horses

So [France's] Charles V nicknamed the German tongue.
—Henry Frederic Reddall's *Fact, Fancy, and Fable*, 1889

Let Them Eat Bread

Medieval texts indicate that a curious confection called *horse-bread* was commonly prepared for horses. This coarse mixture of bran, alfalfa, beans, vegetable trimmings, fodder and what-have-you was concocted by bakers to enliven and strengthen horses much as oats do today. This equine dietary supplement was formed into "great household peck loaves" before baking. Despite its original intention, horse-bread was also quietly mixed into soups and stews, and discreetly served to unsuspecting travelers by innkeepers. This practice became so widespread that a purity law of Edward III mandated that it be served exclusively to horses, and made "only of beans and peas, without other mixture."

An old explanation for how the coarse bread, *pumpernickel*, received its name was that Napoleon, on sampling this Prussian staple, dubbed it in French, "pain pour Nicole," literally bread for his mare, Nicole. Unfortunately for the story, pumpernickel, which translated roughly from German as "devil's flatulence" (from *pumpern*, to break wind) dates back into the 1600s — well before Napoleon's time.

grecianize

To play the Grecian; to speak Greek. *Grecize*, to translate into Greek.
—Rev. John Boag's *Imperial Lexicon of the English Language*, c. 1850

What is an Inkhorn Term?

Greek- and Latin-based "inkhorn terms," abundantly coined beginning in the 1400s, were so called from their association with an ink container, originally made of horn and carried by scribes. In 1553, scholar Thomas Wilson finished *The Arte of Rhetorique*, which was intended to help budding poets develop their craft. The book lampooned the unnecessary use of pompous inkhornisms, offering such ridiculous examples of gibberish as, "I cannot but celebrate and extoll your magnifical dexterity above all others. For how could you have adepted such illustrate prerogative and dominical superiority if the fecundity of your ingeny had not been so fertile and wonderful pregnant?"

The 27-letter inkhornism "honorificabilitudinitatibus"—a 13-syllable monstrosity unleashed in Thomas Nashe's *Lenten Stuffe* (1599), meaning "worthiness of honor" — was once the longest English word. But in the late 1700s, it was surpassed by the 29-letter abomination "floccinaucinihilipilification," a noun which deemed something to be worthless. In the late 19th century, "antidisestablishmentarianism" fell one letter short of the record.

knight of the grammar

A schoolmaster.

—Albert Hyamson's *Dictionary of English Phrases*, 1922

Knight of the pen, a clerk or author.

—Sir James Murray's *New English Dictionary*, 1909

Better Speech Week

In *The American Language* (1936), H. L. Mencken (shown here) recalled a well-intentioned but ill-fated movement to improve American English: "Multitudes of American pedagogues still believe that the natural growth of the language is wild and wicked, and that it should be regulated according to rules formulated in England. To this end they undertake periodical crusades against bad grammar. In 1915, the National Council of Teachers of English — following that hopeful American custom which gave the nation Mother's Day and Safety-First and Eat More Cheese Weeks — proposed to make the first seven days of November Better Speech Week.

"Some of the schoolma'ams, despairing of effecting a wholesale reform, concentrated their efforts upon specific crimes, and among subsidiary weeks thus launched were Ain't-less Week and Final-G Week. They also established a Tag Day, and hung derisory tags on youngsters guilty of such indecencies as *It's me*."

walkist

One who participates in a walking match.

—William Craigie's *Dictionary of American English*, 1940

As soon as the door is once opened to such abominations by those who ought to be the guardians of the language, a host of similar terms make a lodgment. Hence no sooner had men's ears become somewhat accustomed to hear a pedestrian called a *walkist* than the man whose rifle brought down the largest amount of game became a *shootist*.

—M. Schele de Vere's *Americanisms: The English of the New World*, 1872

Instant Nouns

The suffix -*ist* has been arbitrarily added to many expressions, creating durable nouns. *Chemist, biologist* and *physicist*, for example, are still used, but *carpentist* and *plumbist* never were. Likewise, *bicyclist* thrives, but *swimmist, climbist* and *hikist* have vanished. The -*ist* ending was readily adopted by the arts and sciences, leading to such long-lived terms as *dramatist* and *scientist*, although *composuist, mathematist, photographist* and *camerist* fell by the wayside, and *sculptist, writist, dancist, paintist* and *poetist* never existed. The musical realm became a haven for -ist terms, giving rise to violinist, bassist, and more than a dozen others. But fortunately, a few notable exceptions — *tubaist, conductist* and *singist* among them — were not meant to be.

square dinkham

True, straightforward, correct.

—Edward Fraser's *Soldier and Sailor Words and Phrases*, 1925

America's Most Recognizable Expression

In 1839, the common American expression "O.K." was first used by the *Boston Post*. Curiously, it used O.K. as an abbreviation for "oll korrect" in reporting on the local Anti-Bell-Ringing Society, which strove to prohibit dinner bells. Waggish journalists writing in city newspapers from New York to New Orleans then began using this and other intentionally incorrect initials facetiously, such as "K.G." for "no go," "K.Y." for "no use," "O.W." for "all right," and later "K.O." for "commanding officer."

A year later, O.K. became an election slogan and a symbol of the Democratic party, boosting the term's popularity. Supporters of Martin Van Buren referred to themselves as "the O.K. Club" because their candidate was born in Old Kinderhook in New York's Hudson River Valley. Seven decades later, President Woodrow Wilson felt so sure that O.K. was derived from the Choctaw word "okeh" that he took the time to spell it out as such. But not until 1963 did American wordsmith Allen Walker Read solve the mystery of O.K.'s origins. In the meantime, it had become the most familiar of all Americanisms, and it is now heard worldwide.

⫴ undisprovable ⫴

Not to be disproved or excepted against.
— John Kersey's *New English Dictionary*, 1772

Bettermost, best. *Biggermost,* biggest.
—Francis Taylor's *The Folk-Speak of South Lancashire*, 1901

Nethermost, the lowest of all.
—John Kersey's *New English Dictionary*, 1772

How Many Wrongs Make a Right?

Even an English teacher will admit that a few double-negatives, including *unstoppable,* have survived the test of time, while most, such as *undeflowered,* fortunately have not. But in general, most double negatives are best avoided in formal writing. In the same vein, Samuel Pegge's *Anecdotes of the English Language* (1844) offered some unsavory unions of adjectives with awkward intensifiers: "As to *worser,* it is no more than a double comparative with the usual termination, in a case which the ear will bear and which it would abhor in other

 words, such as *better-er, happier-er, sooner-er.* Londoners are farther accused of inflaming the offence by sometimes saying *more worser.* But to shew how much the comparatives, with the auxiliary term *more,* were once allowable, the following examples [from Shakespeare] shall suffice: 'I am *more better* than Prospero' (*The Tempest*); 'more sharper than your swords' (*Henry V*); and 'the envy of *less happier* lands' (*Richard II*)."

ensmall

To condense; a factitious word modeled on *enlarge*.

—John Farmer's *Americanisms, Old and New*, 1889

The Term "Americanism" Is Born

In 1781, Scottish-born clergyman, president of Princeton, and signer of the Declaration of Independence John Witherspoon, the first person to actively collect Americanisms as such, coined the word "Americanism" to denote those expressions he had been squirreling away. In the *Pennsylvania Journal and Weekly Advertiser,* he described them as being a "use of phrases or terms, or a combination of sentences, even among persons of rank and education, different from the use of the same terms or phrases, or the construction of similar sentences in Great Britain."

He went on to say, "It does not follow in every case that the terms or phrases used are worse in themselves, but merely that they are of American and not of English growth. The word *Americanism,* which I have coined for the purpose, is exactly similar in its formation and signification to the word *Scotticism.*" Witherspoon once remarked, "The vulgar in America speak much better than the vulgar in Great Britain for a very obvious reason, that being much more unsettled, and moving frequently from place to place, they are not so liable to local peculiarities, either in accent or phraseology."

Health, Medicine and the Body

The art of Medicine consists in amusing the patient while Nature cures the disease.

—Voltaire (1694–1778), French philosopher and writer

anthropotomist

One who studies human anatomy.

—Sir James Murray's *New English Dictionary*, 1888

One who cuts up or dissects a man; [from Greek] *anthropos*, man, and *tomis* or *tomeus*, one who cuts.

—Edward Lloyd's *Encyclopædic Dictionary*, 1895

Laughter is the Best Medicine

Henri de Mondeville (c. 1260–c. 1320) was among the most innovative surgeons and anatomists of the Middle Ages. He established a medical teaching center in Montpellier, France, studied philosophy and theology, and was an early advocate of the power of positive thinking. Nearly seven centuries before Western medicine would embrace the importance of a patient's mental state as part of the healing process, Mondeville's *Treatise on Surgery* (1316) advised: "Let the surgeon take care to regulate the whole regimen of the patient's life for joy and happiness, allowing his relatives and special friends to cheer him, and by having someone tell him jokes."

Beyond this, Mondeville suggested, "Keep up the spirits of your patients with the music of the viol and the psaltry, by forging letters telling of the deaths of his enemies, or if he be religious, by informing

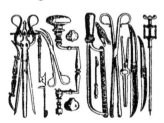

him that he's been made a bishop." In the same work, he scoffed at his less gifted colleagues, declaring, "More surgeons know how to cause suppuration than how to heal a wound."

spleeny

Ill-tempered; peevish. "I know her for a *spleeny* Lutheran."
Henry VIII.

—Rev. Alexander Dyce's *Glossary to the Works of Shakespeare*, 1902

Kidney, temperament, nature, constitution. "Think of that,
a man of my *kidney*." Shakespeare's *Merry Wives of
Windsor* (1598).

— Sir James Murray's *New English Dictionary*, 1901

Emotions of the Spleen

Before the 16th century, physicians and anatomists could only guess
about the functions of some bodily organs, including the spleen. We
find, for example, that *spleenful* was used as an adjective meaning
"passionate" from the idea that laughter and temperament originated
with the spleen, as we hear from Armando in *Love's Labour's Lost*:
"By virtue, thou enforcest laughter; thy silly thought, my spleen." In
this regard, John Donne wrote in 1631, "Laughter is the [hiccup] of
a foolish spleen." This organ was also blamed for "splenitive" mood
swings, depression, melancholy, anger, and moroseness, and gave
rise to a popular expression, "venting
one's spleen." Similarly, Shakespeare
developed the character of Hotspur in
Henry IV, who was "governed by a spleen,"
and wrote in *Henry VIII*: "Your heart is
cramm'd with arrogancy, *spleen* and pride."
Stomachfull was a companion word of the
same era. But today the only organ still regarded
as a seat of emotions is the heart.

clyten

An unhealthy appearance, especially in children. *Clytenish*,
sickly; pale; unhealthy looking.

—John Akerman's *Glossary of Provincial Words and*
Phrases in Wiltshire, 1842

The Advent of Corn Flakes

In 1906, William Kellogg formed the Battle Creek Toasted Cornflake
Company. This company turned out the cereal that his elder brother
John Harvey (shown here) had developed for an elderly patient of
his, who had broken her teeth chewing his zwieback biscuits and
was demanding compensation. John's Battle Creek Sanitarium,
which accommodated the likes of Teddy Roosevelt and John D.
Rockefeller, offered an array of approaches to health. These ranged
from reasonable modes of diet, exercise, sleep and dress, to regular
colonic irrigations, with which John Harvey began each day, and
bizarre electrotherapy devices for reducing men's libido. Regarding
this, Dr. Kellogg knowingly reminded his male patients, "An erection
is nothing but a flagpole on your grave, sir."

A comic spoof of Kellogg's rehabilitation
retreat, the "San," was offered up in the 1994
movie, *The Road to Wellville*, the title of a
pamphlet written for rival cereal-maker C.
W. Post, which claimed that it possessed
"the peculiar power of healing the sick
while being read." Beginning in 1898,
this write-up was included in packages
of Post's Grape-Nuts.

saltimbanco

A quack; [from] Italian *saltare in banco*, to mount the bench.
—Noah Webster's *American Dictionary of the English Language*, 1828

James Graham's Celestial Bed

In 1770, Scottish con man James Graham (1745–1794) emigrated to
Philadelphia, where he set up shop as a "sexologist." There he raised
eyebrows and made serious money by charging £50 for infertile couples
to sleep in his nine-by-twelve "Magnetico-Electrico Bed," which was
fitted with statues of Cupid and Psyche and a battery of magnets.

Graham's *Sketch, or Short Description of Dr. Graham's Medical
Apparatus* (1780) set the scene: "It is placed in a spacious room to the
right of my orchestra, which produces celestial fire and vivifying
influence. This brilliant Celestial Bed is supported by six massive
brass pillars with Saxon blue and purple satin, perfumed with Arabian
spices in the style of the seraglio of a grand Turk. Any gentleman
and his lady desirous of progeny and wishing to spend an evening in
the Celestial Apartment, which coition may, on
compliment of a £50 bank note, be permitted
to partake of the heavenly joys it affords by
causing immediate conception, accompanied
by the soft music. Superior ecstasy which
the parties enjoy in the Celestial Bed
is really astonishing and never before
thought of in this world. The barren
must certainly become fruitful when
they are powerfully agitated in the
delights of love."

calenture

A distemper peculiar to sailors in hot climates wherein they imagine the sea to be green fields, and they throw themselves into it if not restrained.

—Samuel Johnson's *Dictionary of the English Language*, 1755

A species of furious delirium to which sailors are subject in the torrid zone; a kind of phrenitis, the attack of which comes on suddenly after a broiling day.

—Robley Dunglison's *Dictionary of Medical Science*, 1844

From French *calenture*, heat; from Latin *caleo*, to be hot.

—John Ridpath's *Home Reference Library*, 1898

Going Overboard

This bizarre but apparently not uncommon physical and psychological condition broadened in meaning to include fevers on land, and came to denote a passionate desire to act on one's hallucinations, as well as pangs of conscience, and even "baneful lust." In 1719, Daniel Defoe wrote in *Robinson Crusoe*, "In this voyage I had my misfortunes too, particularly that I was continually sick, being thrown into a violent calenture by the excessive heat of the climate." In 1721, Jonathan Swift wrote in "The South-Sea Project":

So, by a calenture misled,
The mariner with rapture sees,
On the smooth ocean's azure bed,
Enamell'd fields and verdant trees.

medicinal days

The sixth, eighth, tenth, twelfth, etc. days of a disease, so called because, according to Hippocrates . . . medicine may be safely administered.

—Ebenezer Brewer's *Dictionary of Phrase and Fable*, 1898

Montaigne on Medicine

French philosopher Michel de Montaigne (1533–1592), whose personal motto became "Que sais-je?" ("What do I know?"), satirized aristocrats and the many quacks and mountebanks around him who were guilty of what he called "supercelestial thought and subterranean conduct." He ridiculed the stern-looking physicians of his day because many superstitiously dispensed their expensive but useless pills in odd numbers; insisted on specific "medicinal days" for swallowing those pills, potions and electuaries (as mentioned above), gathered their herbs at particular hours of the day, and prescribed such ridiculous oddities as "the left foot of a tortoise, the liver of a mole, and blood drawn from under the wing of a white pigeon."

Montaigne (shown here) once wrote mockingly of an unnamed contemporary doctor, who had declared, "Above all things, next to grammar, a physician must surely have his astronomy to know how, when, and at what time every medicine ought to be administered." Montaigne remarked in one of his essays, "Many a man has been a wonder to the world whose wife and valet have seen nothing in him that was even remarkable."

scrofula

A coin given by the sovereigns of England to those whom they touched for the cure of scrofula, or the kingsevil.

—Edward Lloyd's *Encyclopædic Dictionary*, 1895

The Curious Treatment of Scrofula

who was invoked to remedy scrofula, another name for kingsevil.

George Wood's health manual, *Vitalogy: Food Remedies for All Diseases* (1896) listed a questionable cause of, and cure for, scrofula: "There can be no doubt that hereditary predisposition goes before all others, occasioned by tobacco-smoking on the part of the father." His remedy was even less likely: "A few years ago, a distinguished western millionaire wrote of a favorite remedy for scrofulous ulcers. I have never heard of a case where it did not effect a speedy cure, and it can in no case do any injury. In several cases where it has been put to old sores, it has also speedily effected perfect cures. Put one ounce of aquafortis in a bowl or saucer; drop in two copper cents; it will effervesce, leave the cents in; when the effervescence ceases, add two ounces of strong vinegar. The fluid will be of a dark green color. It should and will smart. If too severe, put in a little rain-water. Apply to the sore morning and evening with a soft brush."

Thomas Macaulay's authoritative *History of England* (1849) reported that Charles II touched 92,107 subjects during his reign with no results reported.

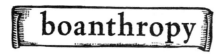

boanthropy

A form of madness in which a man believes himself to be an ox.

—Sir James Murray's *New English Dictionary*, 1888

Cow-tongued, Having a tongue smooth on one side and rough on the other, as purpose serves.

—John Greaves Nall's *Glossary of the East Anglian Dialect*, 1866

Bovine Dilemmas

Robert Chambers's *Book of Days* (1864) examined "ruminating men," including one "who actually chews the cud like an ox. He has many extraordinary properties, being eminent for strength and possessing a set of ribs and sternum very worthy the attention of anatomists. . . . He can reject meals from his stomach at pleasure, and did absolutely, in the course of two hours, go through the whole operation of eating, masticating, swallowing, and returning by the mouth a large piece of bread and a peach. . . . I suppose his ruminating moments are spent in lamenting the peculiarities of his frame."

Paisipae, the wife of Crete's King Minos, was said to have contracted a form of boanthropy, fallen in love with a bull, and bore him a highly illegitimate son. Samuel Butler referenced this in his satire, *Hudibras* (1663-78):

> *This made the beauteous queen of Crete*
> *To take a town-bull for her sweet;*
> *And from her greatness stoop so low,*
> *To be the rival of a cow.*

keach

Uneasiness of mind arising from too great anxiety about domestic affairs or hurry and pressure of business of any sort.
—John Jamieson's *Etymological Dictionary of the Scottish Language*, 1808

Vagitus, the distressing cry of persons under surgical operations.
—Robert Hooper's *Compendious Medical Dictionary*, 1798–1839

Profile of Edgar "Painless" Parker

(1871–1951), a flamboyant American dentist (shown here), who built a $3,000,000-a-year dental empire. After finishing dental school in the mid-1890s, he began practicing on the streets of New York, pulling teeth in a horse-drawn wagon while his brass band attracted spectators and a drum muffled the groans of anguished patients. He then moved on to Canada and Alaska, before overseeing a thirty-office operation headquartered in San Francisco. He admired the unabashed, self-promoting style of P. T. Barnum, and physically resembled fried-chicken king Colonel Sanders.

Calling him "a menace to the dignity of the profession," Parker was denounced by the American Dental Association and many of

his colleagues. In his offices, the self-styled "tooth-plumber" kept wooden buckets filled with yanked teeth, a specimen of which is still displayed at Temple University's dental museum in Philadelphia. Parker claimed to have extracted 357 teeth in a single day and celebrated his achievement with typical panache — having the molars, incisors and canines strung into a long necklace which he sometimes wore in his office.

tar-water

A cold infusion of tar in water, which was formerly a celebrated remedy for many chronic affectations.

—John Ogilvie's *Comprehensive English Dictionary*, 1865

The Miracle of Tar-Water

In the early 1740s, Irish-born bishop, philosopher, mathematician, and poet George Berkeley (1685–1753) discovered the properties of tar-water, which was supposedly instrumental in his recovery from colic, and which he considered a panacea for a host of maladies. He published two treatises, including his last work, *Further Thoughts on Tar-Water*, on the virtues of this substance, the antiseptic properties of which were embraced by America's medical profession into the 20th century. In fact, W. C. Sydney declared in *England and the English in the 18th Century*, "No remedy was more popular during the second half of the eighteenth century than tar-water."

Berkeley's "recipe" for tar-water was outlined in a letter written by attorney John Whishaw in 1744: "His way of making it is to put, I think, a gallon of water to a quart of tar, and after stirring it together, to let it stand forty-eight hours, and then pour off the clear and drink a glass of about half a pint in ye morn, and as much at five in ye afternoon. So it's become [as] common to call for a glass of tar-water in a coffee-house as a dish of tea or coffee."

trollibags

The intestines. Norfolk. [Still known in Northern England.]
—William Holloway's *Dictionary of Provincialisms*, 1838

An exclamation of surprise: "Oh my tripes and *trolly-bags*!"
—William Dickinson's *Glossary of Cumberland*, 1881

Benjamin Franklin's Oddest Idea

In his bluntly titled essay, "Fart Proudly," inventor and Renaissance man Benjamin Franklin proposed a naïve but rational solution to the age old dilemma of releasing intestinal gas: "Were it not for the odiously offensive smell accompanying such escapes, polite people would probably be under no more restraint in discharging such wind in company than they are which spitting or in blowing their noses. My prize question therefore should be to discover some drug, wholesome and not disagreeable, to be mixed with our common food or sauces that shall render our natural discharges of wind from our

bodies not only inoffensive but as agreeable as perfumes. . . . We have the power of changing by slight means the smell of another discharge, that of our water. A few stems of asparagus eaten shall give our urine a disagreeable odour; and a pill of turpentine no bigger than a pea shall bestow on it the pleasing smell of violets. And why should it be thought more impossible in nature to find means of making a perfume of our wind than of our water?"

Adam's leather

The human skin.

—William Craigie's *Dictionary of American English*, 1940

Fornpeckles, freckles.

—Thomas Wright's *Dictionary of Obsolete and Provincial English*, 1857

What To Do About Freckles?

An anonymous self-help health manual, *The Cottage Physician* (1899), offered the following advice to readers troubled with freckles: "Persons affected by these unsightly disorders may remove them without using cosmetics by merely stimulating the absorbent vessels of the skin to take them up and carry them away. Any smart stimulant will assist in this way, but it has been found that the safest are from the vegetable kingdom. One of the best and easiest is Withering's cosmetic lotion, which is made up of a cupful of soured milk and a small quantity of horseradish. . . . Use it to wash the parts affected twice or thrice a day."

Culpepper's *Complete Herbal* (1653) mentioned this approach to facial care: "The distilled water [of feverfew] takes away freckles and other spots and deformities in the face." The anonymous book, *The Complete Cook* (1671) added another cure: "To take away freckles . . . steep a piece of copper in the juice of lemon till it be dissolved, and anoint the place with a feather, morning and evening, washing it off with white wine."

next the heart

All medicine should be taken "next the heart," which means, in the dialect of Suffolk, that the best time for taking medicine is in the morning, fasting.

—Eveline Gurdon's *Suffolk County Folklore,* 1893

Perpetual Pill-Popper

William Hone's *Every-day Book, or Everlasting Calendar of Popular Amusements* (1827) profiled the demise of England's most ravenous consumer of supplements on record, which occurred on in 1817: "Mr. Samuel Jessup, an opulent grazier of pill-taking memory ... died at Heckington [Lincolnshire] aged sixty-five. In twenty-one years, from 1791 to 1816, the deceased took 226,934 pills supplied by a respectable apothecary at Bottesford, which is at the rate of 10,806 pills a year, or twenty-nine pills each day. But as the patient began with a more moderate appetite and increased it as he proceeded in the last five years preceding 1816 he took pills at the rate of seventy-eight a day, and in the year 1814 he swallowed not less than 51,590 [and] 40,000 bottles of mixtures, juleps, and electuaries."

Just before his death, the well-to-do Mr. Jessup ironically appeared as a defendant in a lawsuit charging him with failing to pay his apothecary, a Mr. Wright. As evidence, Wright offered "fifty-five closely written columns" of his notebook, cataloguing the above-mentioned medicines over the years.

whacker

Something large, as a stout man is said to be a *whacker*.
Hampshire and Sussex.

—William Holloway's *Dictionary of Provincialisms*, 1838

Death of a Great Man

In 1809, England's most corpulent man to date, Leicester's 5' 11",
739-pound Daniel Lambert (shown here) died sporting a 112-inch
waistline at age 38. According to contemporary accounts Lambert
began to swell in earnest at about age 21, and within two years the odd
celebrity had reached 450 pounds. In 1806 he reluctantly exhibited
himself at London's Picadilly Circus, but soon grew weary of gawking
spectators and returned home.

One voyeur reported, "When sitting he appears to be a stupendous
mass of flesh for his thighs are so covered by his belly that nothing
but his knees are to be seen, while the flesh of his legs, which
resemble pillows, projects in such a manner as to nearly bury his
feet." Still an attraction, his vest and other personal effects may be
seen in the Newarke Houses Museum in Leicester and the Stamford
Museum in Lincolnshire. Lambert inspired
the short-lived noun *lambert*, meaning to
become oversized, as well as tributes from
several writers. Among them, Herbert
Spencer referred to someone flatteringly
as "a Daniel Lambert of learning," and
George Meredith described London as
"the Daniel Lambert of cities."

vapours

Belonging to or full of vapours. *Vaporous*, in a physical sense, fits of the mother, or melancholy; a disease.

—John Kersey's *New English Dictionary*, 1772

In Physick a distemper vulgarly called "the hypo."

—Thomas Dyche's *New General English Dictionary*, 1740

Treating the Vapours

The term "vapours" was used in Britain as a euphemism for intestinal gas, beginning about the 1420s. The *Oxford English Dictionary* defined *vapours*, "in older medical use," as "exhalations supposed to be developed within the organs of the body, especially the stomach, and to have an injurious effect upon the health." Daniel Defoe's *Robinson Crusoe* (1719), for example, included "*vapours* from an empty stomach." Over the next two centuries, *vapours* came to mean "a morbid condition supposed to be caused by the presence of such exhalations; depression of spirits, hypochondria, hysteria, or other nervous disorder; common 1665–1750." As per the *OED* which added, "So, *the vapours*; common in the 18th century." At that time, fretful upper-class women treated and avoided these psychosomatic conditions by donning heavy petticoats and underwear which they thought would disguise and absorb their bodies' offgassing.

errhine

A medicine which when applied to the mucous membrane of the nose increases the natural secretions and produces sneezing. Having the action of an errhine.

—Sydenham Society's *Lexicon of Medicine and Allied Sciences*, 1897

A remedy whose action is [in] exciting sneezing and increas[ing] discharge.

—Robley Dunglison's *Dictionary of Medical Science*, 1844

Nothing to Sneeze At

Errhine described liquified medications which were steeped into plugs of "lint" before nasal insertion, as well as those *snoached*, or inhaled dry, or sometimes blown into the nose by a doctor using a quill or pipe, to increase secretions. Another practitioner employing errhines was the midwife, who induced sneezing during child delivery as a technique to facilitate a pushing action in the mother.

During the 19th century, "nasal douches" composed of various ingredients were used as a remedy for colds and influenza, as well as their prevention, just as Nicholas Culpepper's *The English Physitian* (1653) had recommended two centuries earlier for more general purposes: "Snuff up the juice of red beet-root; it will cleanse not only the nose, but also the head. This is a singular remedy for such as are troubled with hard congealed stuff in their nostrils."

Love, Courtship and Marriage

Niagara Falls is the second greatest disappointment that an American bride experiences on her honeymoon.

—Oscar Wilde, February, 1882, after visiting the falls

blushet

A young modest girl.

—Rev. John Boag's *Imperial Lexicon of the English Language*, c. 1850

Making Costume Study Respectable

Between the early-1920s and late-1950s, James Laver became known as "the man who made the study of costume respectable" during his tenure as a curator of London's Victoria and Albert Museum. His *Manners and Morals in the Age of Optimism, 1848–1914* (1966) discussed a variety of flirting opportunities in Britain, including "the flirt who had plain sisters," the "tourist flirt," and even the "ecclesiastical flirt." The "regimental flirt" (depicted here) interacted with military officers and coyly pretended to admire their "startling clothes, their mustaches and eyeglasses, [and] the odour of the choice cigars they smoked [and its] tantalizing effect upon their senses." The "seaside flirt" realized that "a sail in a small boat in rough water affords opportunities for the exhibition of nerve and nautical knowledge, while a fishing-party by torchlight leads to so many nice things in the way of huddlings together under one tarpaulin, little screams when the boat rocks, delighted exclamations and . . . the privilege of appearing to lose one's balance and needing the prop of a stalwart arm." Laver concluded, "Etiquette, which would be shocked at Miss Jill and Mr. Jack walking up and down an hotel corridor for an hour at midnight, can look on unmoved at a moonlight promenade on the deck of a yacht, even if it extends far into the small hours."

piscatorian

One who seeks or gains favor with a teacher by being officious toward him. This word was much used in the year 1822, and for a few years after. It is now very seldom heard. From the *piscator*, a fisherman.

—Benjamin Hall's *Collection of College Words and Customs*, 1856

British Wedding Customs

Sir Charles Igglesden's *Those Superstitions* (1931) presented a group of lost British Isles wedding ceremonies in which the groom's livelihood was saluted: "It is recorded how the carpenter's journey from the church door to the roadway was strewn with wooden chips. Along the coast it was customary for the fisherman and his bride to walk over nets. The path of the blacksmith bridegroom was strewn with horseshoes and pieces of old iron, and in the villages of hop-growing counties hops were placed along the footpath of a hop-grower as he left the church with his bride. One can visualize the awkward emblems of other callings, such as the butcher and his bride stepping over roast beef and mutton-chops, or an iron-monger painfully escaping from nails turned upwards. And there was the fishmonger bridegroom treading over slippery fish which had been affected by the heat of the sun. A baker went so far as to wade through flour. A tanner passed over the skins of oxen and sheep — cured, let us hope."

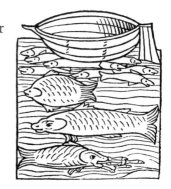

bachelor's wife

The ideal wife, of which a bachelor theorizes or dreams.
—Sir James Murray's *New English Dictionary*, 1888

To *hang out the besom*, to have a fling when your wife is gone on a visit. To be a quasi-bachelor once more.
—Ebenezer Brewer's *Dictionary of Phrase and Fable*, 1898

Choosing a Good Wife

William Cecil, Lord Burghley (1520–1598) conveyed the art of wife selection in his *Precepts and Directions for the Well Advice of a Man's Life* in the days before divorce was common among the masses: "When it shall please God to bring thee to man's estate, use great providence and inspection in choosing thy wife, for from thence shall spring all thy fortune — good or evil. It is an action of life like unto a stratagem of war, wherein a man can err but once. If thy estate be good, match near home and at leisure; if weak, far off and quickly. Inquire diligently of her disposition and how her parents have been inclined in their youth. Let her not be poor, how generous soever, for a man can buy nothing in the market with gentility. Nor choose

a base and uncomely creature altogether for wealth, for it will cause contempt in others and loathing in thee. Neither make choice of a dwarf or a fool, for by one thou shalt beget a race of pygmies. The other will be thy continual disgrace, and it will irke thee to hear her talk."

married all o'er

Said of women who after their marriages become . . . miserable-looking.

—Georgina Jackson's *Shropshire Word-Book*, 1879

Opentyde

was a period lasting from the Feast of Epiphany (January 6) through Ash Wednesday, when marriages commonly took place in Britain. Nuptials were frowned on during Lent, especially on March 19, and were all but forbidden during the Christmas season (late November until Epiphany). June weddings were blessed by the Church, but those during the "lusty month of May" were condemned as a holdover from pagan times, as this old couplet reminds us:

> *Married in May, and kirked [dressed] in green,*
> *Both bride and groom won't long be seen.*

In *Observations on Popular Antiquities* (1813), John Brand noted a custom in the North of England that bordered on indecency, marking the manners of our ancestors. The quote should begin there with "It was for the young men . . . to strive immediately after the ceremony [to see] who could first pluck off the bride's garters from her legs. This was done before the very altar. . . . Whoever were so fortunate as to be victors in this contest — during which the bride was often obliged to scream out and was very frequently thrown down — bore [the garters] about the church in triumph."

deosculate

A kissing with eagerness.

—Edward Phillips's *New World of English Words*, 1658

Osculable, capable of being kissed.

—Sir James Murray's *New English Dictionary*, 1908

Mistletoe Abuse

In 1855, American Author Nathaniel Hawthorne included the following Christmas observation in a journal that was published as his *English Notebooks*: "There were little branches of mistletoe hanging in several parts of our house.... The maids did their utmost to entrap the gentlemen-boarders, old and young, under these privileged places, and there to kiss them, after which they were expected to pay a shilling. It is very queer, being customarily so respectful, that they should assume this license now, absolutely trying to pull the gentlemen into the kitchen by main force, and kissing the harder and more abundantly, the more they were resisted. A little rosy-cheeked lass — at other times very modest — was the most active in this business. I doubt whether any gentleman but myself escaped. I heard old Mr. Smith parleying with the maids last evening, and pleading his age, but he seems to have met with no mercy, for there was a sound of prodigious smacking immediately afterwards."

babies-in-the-eyes

The miniature reflection of himself which a person sees in the pupil of another's eye on looking closely into it. Our old poets make it an employment of lovers to look for them in each other's eyes.

—James Halliwell's *Dictionary of Archaic and Provincial Words*, 1855

Love in the expression of the eyes — the little babe Cupid, and hence the conceit, originating from the reflection of the onlooker in the pupil of another's eyes.

—Ebenezer Brewer's *Dictionary of Phrase and Fable*, 1898

Babies in the eyes is a phrase occurring in our Elizabethan poets.

—John Greaves Nall's *Glossary of the Dialect of East Anglia*, 1866

Bird of the eye, the little refracted image on the retina, or that of a very near spectator reflected. In many languages there [is an] endearing term of this kind. The Greeks call it the *girl* or *virgin*; our ancestors talked of the "baby in the eye."

—Rev. Robert Forby's *Vocabulary of East Anglia*, 1830

The Eyes Have It

An anonymous 17th-century British book of spells suggested, "To know if your husband or wife be bewitched, look well into their eyes, and if you can discern your picture in them they are not bewitched. If you cannot discern your likeness, some person hath bewitched them."

simmiting

An inclination or fondness for a person of the opposite sex; [related to] *simmity*, to look after admiringly, to pay attention to.

—R. Pearse Chope's *Dialect of Hartland, Devonshire*, 1891

Pairing Up in England

Henri Misson wrote in his *Memoirs and Observations in his Travels Over England* (1719), "On the Eve of the 14th of February, St. Valentine's Day, a time when all living Nature inclines to couple, the young folks in England and Scotland too, by a very ancient custom, celebrate a little festival that tends to the same end. An equal number of maids and batchelors get together, each writes their true or some feigned name upon separate billets, which they roll up and draw by way of lots, the maids taking the men's billets, and the men the maids', so that each of the young men lights upon a girl that he calls his Valentine, and each of the girls upon a young man which she calls her's. . . . Fortune having thus divided the company into so many couples, the Valentines give treats to their mistresses, wear their billets several days upon their bosoms or sleeves, and this little sport often ends in love. This ceremony is practised differently in different counties, and according to the freedom or severity of Madam Valentine. There is another kind of Valentine, which is the first young man or woman that chance throws in your way in the street or elsewhere on that day."

dearworth

Precious.

—Herbert Coleridge's *Dictionary of the First, or Oldest Words in the English Language*, 1863

The words [*dear* and *dearest*], curiously enough, have two distinct and opposite meanings. When taken from Anglo-Saxon *derian*, it means to hate, and from the Scottish *dere*, to annoy. It is in this sense that Shakespeare wrote in *Hamlet*: "Would that I had met my dearest foe in Heaven."

—Edwin Radford's *Unusual Words and How They Came About*, 1946

New York Valentine's Day Custom

Writing in *Colonial Days of Old New York* (1896), Alice Earle offered a curious Valentine's Day observance among early Dutch settlers called Vrouwne dagh, or *Women's day*: "Every young girl sallied forth in the morning armed with a heavy cord with knotted end. She gave every young man whom she met several smart lashes with the knotted cord. Perhaps these were 'love-taps,' and were given with no intent of stinging. Judge Egbert Benson wrote in 1816 that in New York this custom dwindled to a similar Valentine observance by children when the girls chased the boys with many blows. In one school the boys asked for a *Mannen dagh* [Man Day] with which to repay the girls' stinging lashes." This custom may have commemorated the martyrdom of St. Valentine, who was beaten with sticks in about 270 AD.

bachelor's fare

Bread, cheese, and kisses.

—Albert Hyamson's *Dictionary of English Phrases*, 1922

Kissing Friday

On the Friday immediately following Shrove Tuesday, English schoolboys were once entitled to kiss any of the girls in their classes without fear of punishment or rejection — a custom that continued at least as late as the 1940s. Horton Cooper's *North Carolina Mountain Folklore and Miscellany* (c. 1972) reported these rules involving schoolchildren: "Boys shall not carry any girls in their arms or on their backs unless heavy rains or mush ice have made the creeks and branches impossible to cross, and then only boys who are barefoot or wearing boots may do so. No hugging, squeezing, or kissing shall take place while the girl is being transported across the water." Elsewhere, Cooper mentioned the following superstition involving therapeutic smooching: "Kiss a red-headed person of the opposite sex to cure fever blisters."

Julia Bradley's *Modern Manners and Social Forms* (1889) offered Victorian women advice on expressing affection —or rather *not* doing so: "It is now held by many that the prudent and modest maiden should not even allow her lover, even after their engagement, to kiss her. Not until after marriage should such a favour be granted."

chirology

The art of conversing with the hands and fingers.

—Joseph Worcester's *Dictionary of the English Language*, 1881

Handlanguage, the art of conversing by the hands.

—Rev. John Boag's *Imperial Lexicon of the English Language*, c. 1850

Pepys's Night on the Town

In 1667, London diarist and ladies' man Samuel Pepys described his pleasurable theater evening, lapsing into "diary Franglais" in order to thinly veil a romantic interlude: "I [went] abroad with my wife and little Betty Michell . . . to show them a play, *The Chances*. . . . The whole play pleases me well, and most of all the sight of many fine ladies — among others my Lady Castlemayne and Mrs. Middleton. The latter of the two hath a very excellent face and body, I think. Thence by coach to the New Exchange, and there laid out money, and I did give Betty Michell two pairs of gloves. . . . I was troubled with my pain, having got a bruise on my right testicle, I know not how. But this I did make good use of to make my wife shift sides with me, and I did come to sit avec Betty Michell, and there had her [hand] which elle did give me very frankly, and did hazer whatever I voudrais avec la, which did plaisir me grandement, and so set her at home with my mind mighty glad." When Pepys's lost diary was first published in 1825, this risqué passage was edited out due to the improper moral example it provided.

knotchelled

Then a man publicly declares he will not pay any of his wife's debts which have been contracted since some fixed day, she is said to be *knotchelled*, a certain disgraceful imaginary mark. Lancashire.

—Roger Wilbraham's *Glossary of Some Words Used in Cheshire*, 1826

In short, she is a marked woman.

—Edgerton Leigh's *Words Used in the Dialect of Cheshire*, 1877

In Lancashire, to "cry a woman knotchel" is when a man gives a public notice that he will not pay his wife's debts.

—James Halliwell's *Dictionary of Archaisms and Provincialisms*, 1855

Cry-notchil, to advertise irresponsibility for a wife's debts. In the old time, this was affected by means of the bell-man. It is now done through the medium of newspapers.

—Francis Taylor's *The Folk-Speech of South Lancashire*, 1901

Protecting the Groom

According to a 1784 issue of *Gentlemen's Magazine*, a man could protect himself from his bride's debts with an early, wordless form of prenuptial agreement, "if he takes her from the hands of the priest it is supposed that he will not then be liable for her obligations."

octogamie

Marrying eight times. From Latin *octo*, and Old French *gamie* [marriage].

—Alois Brandl's *Glossary of Middle English Literature*, 1949

Going Once, Going Twice . . .

In 1832, a "wife-sale" was held in Carlisle, Scotland. According to Robert Chambers's *Book of Days* (1864), "It is a prevalent notion amongst the rude and ignorant in England that a man, by setting his wife up to public auction, and so parting with her, legally dissolves the marriage tie and escapes from all its obligations. [Joseph] Thompson, under this belief, came into Carlisle with his wife . . . with a rope, or halter, of straw round her neck . . . and by the bellman announced that he was about to sell her." Despite his original asking price of fifty shillings, Thompson's efforts netted him only twenty and a Newfoundland dog. Afterwards, he and his wife were said to have "parted in perfect good temper."

At that time, divorce was very difficult for the lower classes to obtain, so occasionally a man would offer up his wife to the highest bidder. London's Smithfield Market, where butchered and on-the-hoof meat has been sold since medieval times, was the most popular venue for wife-sales. The practice, never really legal, had its heyday in the 1700s, and was usually done with the wife's consent. The last wife-sale took place in 1887, and the act was not formally abolished until a ruling by the Lord Chancellor accomplished this in 1891.

father-in-church

The person who gives away the bride; used chiefly
by old people.
—Angelina Parker's *Supplement to the Oxfordshire Glossary*, 1881

Enthalamizo, [to] bring the bride and groom to bed.
—Elisha Coles's *An English Dictionary*, 1713

The Wedding Night

French visitor Henri Misson prepared this nuptial narrative in
Memoirs and Observations in his Travels Over England (1719):
"When bedtime is come, the bridemen pull off the bride's garters. . . .
This done, and the garters being fastened to the hats of the gallants,
the bridesmaids carry the bride into the bedchamber, where they
undress her and lay her in bed. The bridegroom, who by the help of
his friends is undressed in some other room, comes in his nightgown
as soon as possible to his spouse, who is surrounded by mother, aunts,
sisters, and friends. . . . The bridemen take the bride's stockings, and
the bridemaids the bridegroom's. . . . While
some amuse themselves agreeably with
these little follies, others are preparing
a good posset . . . a potion made up
of milk, wine, yolks of eggs, sugar,
cinnamon, nutmeg, etc. This they
present to the young couple, who
swallow it down as fast as they can to
get rid of such troublesome company.
The bridegroom prays, scolds, entreats
them to be gone, and the bride says
ne'er a word, but thinks the more."

Children's cries.

—B. E. Gent's *Dictionary of the Termes of the Canting Crew*, c. 1699

Go after, to court; to go sweethearting. "Does John *go after* Mary?"

—G. F. Northall's *Warwickshire Word-Book*, 1896

Sitting Up on Saturday Night

Christina Hole's *Traditions and Customs of Cheshire* (1937) described a questionable practice known as "sitting-up" in Barthomley, which was deeply deplored by the clergy: "On Saturday nights, the courting couples met and spent the night together in the house or the outbuildings, which were left unlocked for them. All attempts to stop them were unsuccessful since farmers could not get any servants to come to them on hiring-days unless this privilege was allowed. The custom was by no means confined to Barthomley, but was found all over Cheshire and the counties bordering it. It probably did very little harm, and resembles somewhat a custom found in Finland. There the young man was admitted to the girl's room and was allowed to take off his boots and coat before lying down, but no more. The utmost censure would have been visited by public opinion on any young man who abused his privilege, and in fact few ever did."

Royalty, Aristocrats and Rogues

It is better to die a king than to live a prince.

—Napoleon Bonaparte, king of France, to his brother
Louis Bonaparte, who attempted to decline Napoleon's offer
to make him king of Holland in 1806. (See page 61.)

chuffy

Naughty, proud, puffed up; fat and fleshy. In some parts, clownish.

—M. A. Courtney's *Glossary of Words in Use in Cornwall*, 1880

Fussy, proud, conceited.

—Sidney Addy's *Glossary of Words Used in the Neighbourhood of Sheffield*, 1888

A Profile of King James I

In 1603, James I (shown here, outfitted for falconry) ascended the English throne. In his *History of England* (1848–1861), historian Thomas Macaulay wrote disparagingly of him and of this date: "James was always boasting of his skill in what he called *kingcraft*; and yet it is hardly possible even to imagine a course more directly opposed to all the rules of kingcraft than that which he followed. . . . He enraged and alarmed his Parliament by constantly telling them that they held their privileges merely during his pleasure, and that they had no more business to inquire what he might lawfully do than what the Deity might lawfully do. . . . His cowardice, his childishness, his pedantry, his ungainly person and manners, his provincial accent, made him an act of derision. . . . On the day of the accession of James I, our country descended from the rank she had hitherto held and began to be regarded as a power hardly of the second order."

coney

A creature which burroughs and breeds in warrens; a rabbit. From Belgian *konijn*, Italian *coniglio*.

—Daniel Fenning's *Royal English Dictionary*, 1775

All Hail the Rabbit King!

In 1806, Napoleon Bonaparte installed his brother, Louis Bonaparte, as the king of Holland. This came barely a decade after the French decided that they had suffered enough political and financial inequity, and guillotined thousands of aristocrats, royal family members and sympathizers. But Napoleon downplayed all of this by crowning himself emperor in 1804.

The selection of Louis (shown here) was questionable from the onset, in part because he suffered from debilitating depression. As a result, he was unable to make important decisions, such as where to situate the capital, and changed its location a dozen times during his four-year reign, causing his diplomatic corps to complain. Despite his poor command of the Dutch language, he once attempted to endear himself to his new subjects after his coronation, but instead gave his subjects pause — and reason for laughter. Rather than telling them that he was their "Koning van Holland" (king of Holland), he mistakenly referred to himself as the "Konijn van Olland" (*konijn* was related to *coney*, as above), the rabbit of Holland. With this blunder he earned himself the derisive moniker "Rabbit King" for the duration of his reign and beyond.

fen-nightingale

A frog; otherwise called a *March-bird*. It is that month when frogs are vocal.

—Rev. Robert Forby's *Vocabulary of East Anglia*, 1830

Fen-nightingales, toads and frogs, from their continued croaking at night. [From *fen*, swamp.]

—John Camden Hotten's *Slang Dictionary*, 1887

Corresponding with the Queen

In an 1859 letter to the Princess Royal, Queen Victoria expressed these sentiments regarding infants: "An ugly baby is a very nasty object — and the prettiest is frightful when undressed — till about four months; in short, as long as they have their big body and little limbs and that terrible frog-like action."

Annie Randall White's *Twentieth Century Etiquette* (1900) advised her subjects about the proper way to correspond with the queen: "When you write to Queen Victoria the paper you use must be thick and white, and the letter must be put into an envelope large

enough to contain it without folding. A letter which has been folded never reaches the queen, and the chances are that she never hears of its existence. Such letters are dealt with by the Mistress of the Robes who, if she considers them of sufficient importance to be handed to Her Majesty, returns them to their senders with directions as to how the letter should be sent to the sovereign."

wheady

Tedious; wearisome, as a wheady mile, a mile more than what was expected in a journey. Shropshire.

—William Holloway's *Dictionary of Provincialisms*, 1838

Dull music, anything tedious is said to be *dull music*.

—John Farmer's *Americanisms, Old and New*, 1889

The Same Old Thing

France's Henri IV (1553–1610) is traditionally associated with the origin of the curious French expression *toujours perdrix*, which literally means "always partridge," but figuratively indicates something repeated "ad nauseam." Over the years, the king's spiritual adviser grew increasingly critical of His Majesty's lapses into marital infidelity. Weary of being gently browbeaten on the subject, the king ordered that the confessor's favorite delicacy, roast partridge, be served to him morning, noon and night. At first the cleric enjoyed his repasts, and ate them with relish, but eventually he began to find partridge less and less appealing. After several weeks of this same diet, he complained to Henri (shown here) about having to eat the same meal over and over. As planned, the king was only too happy to turn the tables and point out the parallel to the sexual boredom that had led the monarch to pursue more varied fare.

antimonarchical

The quality of being opposed to monarchy.

—Rev. John Boag's *Imperial Lexicon of the English Language*, c. 1850

A Woman of Letters

Celebrated English letter-writer Lady Mary Wortley Montagu (1688–1762) grew up beautiful and intelligent, and possessed a strong interest in reading and writing. Despite her standing in society and marriage to a diplomat, Lady Mary maintained her disdain for the follies of royalty and war, which she bravely expressed in a letter dated July 12, 1744: "I regard almost all quarrels of princes on the same footing, and I see nothing that marks man's unreason so positively as war. Indeed, what folly to kill one another for interests often imaginary, and always for the pleasure of persons who do not think themselves even obliged to those who sacrifice themselves!"

She expressed her disdain for both organized religion and

quackery in a letter dated April 24, 1748: "We have no longer faith in miracles and relics, and therefore with the same fury run after [medical] recipes and physicians. The same money which three hundred years ago was given for the health of the soul is now given for the health of the body, and by the same sort of people — women and half-witted men."

under the rose

The vulgar saying "under the rose" is said to have taken its rise from convivial entertainments . . . when persons desired to confine their words to the company present.

—John Brand's *Observations on Popular Antiquities*, 1841

In many places they have over their own tables a rose painted, and what is spoken *under the rose* must not be revealed.

—Henry Peacham's *The Truth of Our Times*, 1638

A Rose Is a Rose Is a Rose

The still-heard expressions *under the rose* and its Latin forerunner, *sub rosa*, meaning "in secret," draw their origins from Roman and Greek mythologies in which Eros presented a rose to Harpocrates, the god of silence and Cupid employed the rose to influence Harpocrates to remain mum about one of Venus' many amorous indiscretions. *Sub rosa* was adopted into English during Tudor times, when the floral decoration of banquet halls was apt to include carved or painted roses from the many rose gardens. As an additional reminder, a single fresh rose was sometimes suspended from the ceiling above the dinner table, and women would even wear garlands of roses — to suggest to guests that anything uttered there while inebriated was said "under the rose" and so must be kept confidential by all. Pope Clement VII began adorning Church confessionals with carved roses in 1526.

headsman

One who cuts off heads; an executioner.

—Rev. John Boag's *Imperial Lexicon of the English Language*, c. 1850

A Sketch of Peter the Great

(shown here) capricious 6' 7" Russian tsar. Despite having assumed his regal position at age ten, this Renaissance man mastered skills that would have qualified him for perhaps 20 occupations, including barbering, surgery and dentistry. Not surprisingly, his courtiers neglected to mention their ailments to avoid attracting his attention, as he enjoyed pulling teeth and had a number of patients die after surgery. Peter excelled as a shipwright, enjoyed working with lathes, and crafted hundreds of objects, such as model boats, chairs, snuffboxes, medals and crockery. He transformed Russia from a backward, traditional society to a European nation in which the arts and sciences began to flourish.

But his reign was tainted with cruelty and bloodshed. Peter personally executed a number of prisoners with an ax and, fearing

sedition, ordered the torture of his own son Alexis, from which Alexis died. And in perhaps his darkest deed, Peter — who himself had sired many illegitimate children — discovered his wife Catherine had taken palace chamberlain Willem Mons as a lover. Peter had Mons executed and put his head in a jar of alcohol, displaying it in her bedroom for several years.

whileheft

Flattery; deceitfulness. "They *whilehefted* him."

—Margaret Ann Courtnay's *Glossary of Words
in Use in West Cornwall*, 1880

A Portrait of the Queen

James Miller's *Complete Handbook of Etiquette* (c. 1875) contained this anecdote of the "Virgin Queen," which showed her human side: "It has justly been observed that most women will forgive a liberty sooner than a slight. They will always pardon and generally cherish the admiration which is more warm than delicate. They are more pleased with sincerity than offended at ardour. A striking proof of this was furnished in the case of Elizabeth I. When she once gave audience to some deputies from Holland, a young man, on seeing the queen, expressed in very licentious terms his admiration of her personal charms. The ladies-in-waiting, exhibit[ed] great offence at the indelicacy. The queen insisted on knowing what had been said and, far from being offended at the indecorum of his language, she was pleased with its admiration. When the ambassadors were dismissed, each was presented with a chain of gold worth eight hundred crowns. But the gallant who had found the queen so handsome received a chain worth sixteen hundred crowns, which he ever afterwards wore around his neck. The *woman* had overcome the *queen*."

whizz-bang

A mixture of morphine and cocaine injected subcutaneously.

—Maurice Weseen's *Dictionary of American Slang*, 1934

The Mysterious Death of George V

England's official documents describe the death of King George V (shown below) in January 1936 as having been a "peaceful transition" rounded with a sleep at Sandringham Castle, after inquiring about the welfare of the kingdom.

Technically this may have been true, but notes of the king's physician, Lord Dawson, revealed some unexpected facts and royal omissions when they were declassified half a century later. Dawson reported, "At about 11 p.m. it was evident that the last stage [of illness] might endure for many hours, unknown to the patient but little comporting with the dignity and serenity which he most richly merited and which demanded a brief final scene. I therefore decided to determine the end." His Majesty was first numbed with

morphine, but not before the furious monarch reportedly managed to bark his indignant final words, "Damn you!" According to Lord Dawson's journal, the king's death — or perhaps more correctly, his euthanasia — was then hastened with the consent of his wife, Queen Mary, and his son Edward, who immediately became George VI, using a fatal *whizz-bang* of morphine and cocaine.

regicide

A murderer of a king.

—Thomas Dyche's *New General English Dictionary*, 1740

Ludwig Meets Wagner

Ludwig II of Bavaria (shown here) was born in 1845 in Nymphenburg Castle near Munich and was murdered in 1886 by his own ministers after squandering much of the royal treasury. Ludwig's father, King Maximilian II, often took his family on holidays to Hohenschwangau Castle, which he had restored, where the young prince developed a fascination with castles, mountain scenery and swans. In 1861, Ludwig attended his first opera by Richard Wagner, *Lohengrin*, the libretto of which he had memorized. In 1864 he ascended the throne, and with him came his growing obsession with medieval architecture and Wagner's music.

He poured enormous public resources into the construction of several castles, including world-famous Neuschwanstein, after which Disneyland's icon was modeled. Grottoes were included, where Wagner's operas could be watched by Ludwig and his guests from swanlike boats. The monarch neglected his duties of state and began showing other signs of mental imbalance, including rapid weight gain. In desperation, his cabinet and doctor declared the king insane and had him drowned near Berg Castle. Ironically, the money attracted by tourists visiting these castles has greatly exceeded the investment.

unsex

To make otherwise than the sex commonly is.

—Rev. John Boag's *Imperial Lexicon of the English Language*, c. 1850

Come you spirits that tend on mortall thoughts, unsex
me here.

—William Shakespeare's *Macbeth*, 1605

Victoria and the English Woman

Queen Victoria may have been a bedrock of British stability, but she
did precious little to advance the position of women. In March 1870,
for example, she wrote to Sir Theodore Martin about the activities of a
Lady Amberley (1842–1874), who had agitated in support of the rights
of women: "The queen is most anxious to enlist everyone who can
speak or write to join in checking this mad, wicked folly of Women's
Rights, with all its attendant horrors, on which her poor feeble sex is
bent, forgetting every sense of womanly feelings and propriety. Lady
Amberley ought to get a good whipping. Were woman to unsex [see
above] themselves by claiming equality with men, they would become

the most hateful, heathen, and disgusting
of beings." But the queen also wished
she had been born a man so she could
have died in battle, and complained
of women's subservience in marriage.
In 1860, she carped in a letter to the
Princess Royal: "All marriage is such a
lottery . . . though it may be a very happy
one. Still the poor woman is bodily and
morally the husband's slave. That always
sticks in my throat."

slaistering

A term applied to a strong, powerful man.

—F. T. Dinsdale's *Provincial Words Used in Teasdale*, Durham, 1849

In the Days Before Tonsillectomies

George Washington died in 1799 of acute laryngitis just a fortnight before the dawn of the 19th century. Complicating matters, doctors had drained the first president of more than a gallon of blood in one day. At that time, news of his death required ten days to travel less than 200 miles, from the capital, New York, to Boston.

When first asked to become president, Washington lamented, "I call Heaven to witness that this very act would be the greatest sacrifice of my personal feelings and wishes that I ever have been called upon to make. Every personal consideration conspires to rivet me to retirement." His wife Martha, in fact, believed that his untimely death was brought on by his presidency, during which he came to think that the British were planning to reinvade and subjugate their former colonies. In response, Washington's Chief Justice John Jay negotiated an unpopular treaty with London known as "Jay's Treaty," which allowed the British to retain North American military posts and to seize American ships at will. As a result, both Jay and Washington were hated by many countrymen, and "the Father of his Country" became the subject of impeachment bravado and even assassination threats.

abditory

A hiding place.

—William Grimshaw's *Ladies' Lexicon and Parlour Companion,* 1854

Oak Apple Day

celebrates the return of Charles II to London in 1660 — the Restoration. His father, Charles I, dictated the following memoir to Samuel Pepys nine years after successfully hiding from Cromwell's army in an oak tree near Boscobel, Shropshire, following the civil war Battle of Worcester: "Major Carlos . . . told me that it would be very dangerous for me. . . . He knew but one way how to pass the next day, and that was to get up into a great oak in a pretty plain place, where we might see round about us, for the enemy would certainly search at the wood for people that had made their escape. Of which proposition of his I approving, we went and carried up with us some victuals for the whole day — bread, cheese, small beer, and nothing else — and we got up into a great oak that had been lopped some three or four

years before, and being grown out again very bushy and thick, should not be seen through, and here we stayed all day. While we were in this tree we saw soldiers going up and down in the thicket of the wood, searching for persons escaped."

The "Royal Oak" which stands here today has in fact been replanted, as visitors broke off enough of this tree's bark to kill it.

kingdomed

Proud of royalty.
> —Rev. John Boag's *Imperial Lexicon of the English Language*, c. 1850

Superbiloquent, speaking proudly.
> —Elisha Coles's *An English Dictionary*, 1713

A Wistful Farewell to Royalty

English Statesman Edmund Burke lamented the death of Marie Antoinette and her gilded era, writing in his *Reflections on the Revolution in France* (1790), "Little did I dream that I should have lived to see such disasters fallen upon her in a nation of gallant men." Burke continued to gush: "I thought ten thousand swords must have leaped from their scabbards to avenge even a look that threatened her with insult. But the Age of Chivalry is gone. That of sophisters, economists, and calculators has succeeded, and the glory of Europe is extinguished forever. Nevermore shall we behold that generous loyalty to rank and sex, that proud submission, that dignified obedience, that subordination of the heart which kept alive, even in servitude itself, the spirit of exalted freedom. The unbought grace of life, the chief defense of nations, the nurse of manly sentiment and heroic enterprise is gone! It is gone, that sensibility of principle, that chastity of honour, which inspired courage whilst it mitigated ferocity, which ennobled whatever it touched."

Games, Pastimes and Amusements

The bow always bent will quickly break;
But if unstrung will serve your need.
So let the mind relaxation take
To return to its task with fresher heed.

—Phaedrus (c. 15 BC–50 AD)
Roman versifier of *Aesop's Fables*

clock-faces

A favorite name for the small circles of ice formed upon a
pool when it begins to freeze over.

—Francis Taylor's *The Folk-Speech of South Lancashire*, 1901

Shrammed, benumbed or shrunk up with cold.

—W. H. Long's *Dictionary of the Isle of Wight Dialect*, 1886

England's Festive Frost Fairs

have taken place whenever the Thames froze solid, beginning in
January 1564. The reigning monarch herself, who was considered an
excellent archer, attended and chose to "shoot at marks" with a bow and
arrow. John Stow's *Sumarie of Englyshe Chronicles* (1561) described
the fair: "The ice became firme and . . . then all sortes of men, women,
and children went boldly upon the ice in most partes. . . . People were
many that set up boothes and standings upon the ice, as fruit-sellers,
victuallers that sold beere and wine, shoemakers, and a barber's tent."
These chilly gatherings cropped up occasionally during cold
spells through 1814, allowing memorable outdoor
experiences for enterprising shopkeepers
and fun-loving locals. But the previously
broader, shallower, and slower Thames
was narrowed by the 19th-century
Embankment project, creating a
swifter river and reducing its
tendency to freeze.

whisterclister

A stroke or blow under the ear. Devonshire. *Whisterpoop*, a backhanded blow. Exmoor. *Wherret*, a great blow; perhaps a backhanded blow.

—Francis Grose's *Provincial Glossary*, 1811

Handy-pungy, a fight with the fists.

—Thomas Darlington's *The Folk-Speech of South Cheshire*, 1887

Boxing in Britain

In *English Home-Life* (1947), Christina Hole wrote of the British love of rough entertainment during the 17th century: "Boxing was everybody's delight, from village lads sparring at home to young sprigs of nobility who were proud to learn the noble art from the hands of established champions. Public contests attracted enormous crowds who came from all parts to watch the savage fighting without gloves and without the restraints of Queensbury Rules, which were not introduced until the following century. Severe injuries were sometimes suffered by the contestants, but no one minded that. In spite of superficial refinements it was a rough and brutal age, with an almost total indifference to human or animal pain. Great crowds assembled to see a hanging, and windows with a good view were hired by young men of fashion, as they would be today for a coronation."

jeoparty-trot

A quick motion, between running and walking when one, on account of fear or weakness, is not able to run at full speed. The term seems to have had its origin from the flight of those who . . . were often obliged to escape from their enemies.

—John Jamieson's *Etymological Dictionary of the Scottish Language*, 1808

Let the Games Begin

Unethical practices have been an issue for both Olympic and professional athletes since the first Olympic games were held in Olympia, Greece in 776 B.C. Although steroids were not available in ancient Greece, clandestine cheating with magic charms, spells and potions — which have fallen by the wayside due to their ineffectiveness — dates back to the earliest contests. Herbal preparations, such as one made from rocket arugula called the "Semen of Hercules," were sometimes used by athletes until game organizers clamped down, requiring contestants to live in an "Olympic village" and undergo a month of scrutiny before the events.

Records of outlawed magic spells for runners have been found on fragments of papyrus, such as "Hermes's wondrous victory charm."

It attempted to invoke the help of this god of speed, while another to Nike, the goddess of victory, was secretly inscribed on tiny sheets of gold and concealed inside sandals. Amazingly, we still see the Nike logo festooning athletic shoes nearly 2,800 years later.

hobthrust

A local spirit famous for whimsical pranks.

—John Brockett's *Glossary of North Country Words*, 1825

London Pranksters

In London, boys assemble round the inviting shops of the pastrycooks, and dexterously nail the coat-tails of spectators who venture near enough, to the bottoms of the window frames, or pin them strongly together by their clothes. Sometimes eight or ten persons find themselves thus connected. The dexterity and force of the nail-driving is so quick and sure that a single blow seldom fails of doing the business effectually. Withdrawal of the nail without a proper instrument is out of the question, and consequently the person nailed must either leave part of his coat, as a cognizance of his attachment, or quit the spot with a hole in it. At every nailing and pinning, shouts of laughter arose from the perpetrators and the spectators. Yet it often happens to one who turns and smiles at the duress of another that he also finds himself nailed. Efforts at extrication increase mirth; nor is the presence of a constable — who is usually employed to attend and preserve free "ingress, egress, and regress" — sufficiently awful to deter the offenders.

—William Hone's *Every-Day Book or Everlasting Calendar of Popular Amusements*, 1827

proffereth

When a hart entereth a river or a pool, which is termed the *foil*, say *he descendeth*; when you see him ready to enter water, say *he proffereth*; for the second time, *reproffereth*; after you see where he hath trod, the water filling his footsteps, they say "here the hart *defouleth*."

—H. J. Pye's *The Sportsman's Dictionary*, 1807

Alytarch, keeper of order at public sports.

—Elisha Coles's *An English Dictionary*, 1713

And on the Seventh Day They Played

During the 11th year of her reign, in 1569, Queen Elizabeth I issued a "license" regarding Sunday sports in her kingdom. In one enormous sentence of over 200 words of antique legalese, addressed to "all mayors, sheriffs, constables, and other head officers," she specified

which activities qualified "for the preservation of the Queen Majesty's peace." These included "the shooting with the standard, the shooting with the broad arrow, the shooting at the twelve score prick, the shooting at the Turk, the leaping for men, the wrestling, the throwing of the sledge, and the pitching of the bar," along with "all such games as have at any time heretofore or licensed, used, or played."

blonde-bound

Held up by a woman; an excuse for being late on the job.
Pacific Northwest.

—Walter McCulloch's *Woods Words: A Comprehensive
Dictionary of Logger's Terms*, 1958

Old woman's luck, having the wind in one's face both
going and returning. Lincolnshire, Oxfordshire.

—Joseph Wright's *English Dialect Dictionary*, 1898–1905

Brunettes and First Footing

It is still considered important in North Cheshire that the first person
to cross the threshold on New Year's Day shall be a dark-haired man.
A fair man is very unlucky and a red-haired one even more so. A
woman is worse, whatever the colour of her hair. To avoid the risk of
such disastrous visits the master of the house, if he is dark, goes out
just before midnight. As soon as the clock strikes, he is admitted as
the "First Foot." If he happens to be fair, a suitably-coloured friend
does it for him, and in some districts a dark man will go round the
village, being warmly welcomed at every house
as a luck-bringer. He generally carries with
him a piece of bread, a piece of coal, and some
money so that the family shall want neither
food, firing, nor wealth during the year. It was
formerly thought unlucky to let anything be
taken from the house until something had
been brought in. Hence the importance of
First Foot gifts.

—Christina Hole's *Traditions and
Customs of Cheshire*, 1937

gay-cards

The cards in a pack which are painted with figures.
Norfolk [England].

—William Holloway's *Dictionary of Provincialisms*, 1838

Devil's books, playing cards. A Presbyterian phrase used in reproof of the term *king's books*, applied to a pack of cards. From the French *livre des quatre rois*, the *Book of the Four Kings*. Also called the *Devil's Bible*.

—Ebenezer Brewer's *Dictionary of Phrase and Fable*, 1898

Know When to Fold 'Em

In 1628, England's Worshipful Company of Playing-card Makers has annually elected their head officer. Charles Cotton's *The Compleat Gamester* (1674) advised: "Gaming is an enchanting witchery, gotten betwixt idleness and avarice; an itching disease that makes some scratch his head, whilst others, as if they were bitten by a Tarantula, are laughing themselves to death; and it is a paralytic distemper which, seizing the arm, a man cannot chuse but shake his elbow. It hath this ill property above all other vices: that it renders a man

incapable of prosecuting any serious action and makes him unsatisfied with his own condition; he is either lifted up to the top of mad joy with success or plunged to the bottom of despair by misfortune. . . . As he is transported with joy when he wins, so losing he is tost upon the billows of a high swelling passion till he hath lost sight of both sense and reason."

fauxonry

Fraud. Adaptation of Old French *faussoner*, to deceive, *faus*, false.

—Sir James Murray's *New English Dictionary*, 1901

A Profile of William Gilbert ("WG") Grace

legendary English cricketer, who excelled as an amateur for forty-four seasons (1865 to 1908), helping develop the sport with innovative forms of batting, fielding and bowling. Early in his career, before WG (caricatured as the larger figure below) and others began accepting money for playing, amateurism in sports was highly esteemed in Britain, much as some Olympic athletes are today. But with the growth of railways came organized cricket "sides" which could more easily travel about to compete with those of distant towns — a system that needed financial commitment and spectator fees.

Non-professionals often paid for their own transportation, lodgings and meals, and were reimbursed from the admission receipts, and the temptation to cheat naturally arose. English gentlemen's clubs took the amateur status of these players so seriously that Grace was at times forced by these aristocrats to answer charges of having claimed inflated travel expenses, which he likely did. But as a medical doctor with a clinic, WG bore the expense, for example, of hiring substitute doctors when he traveled. He was even accused of amassing more money than professional cricketers.

tripudiation

Dancing.

—Henry Cockeram's *Interpreter of Hard English Words*, 1623

Tripudist, one given to "tripudiating."

—Sir James Murray's *New English Dictionary*, 1919

Polka History

In 1844, the *Illustrated London News* reported on the controversial Bohemian dance craze that developed in the early 1830s and eventually swept across Europe: "It is a waste of time to consider this nonsense. The weathercock heads of the Parisians have been delighted always by any innovation, but they never imported anything more ridiculous or ungraceful than this Polka. It is a hybrid confusion of Scotch lilt, Irish jig, and Bohemian waltz, and need only to be seen once to be avoided forever." The name was from the Czech *pulka*, meaning "half," for the half steps used in it.

But despite its risqué and vulgar reputation, which rivaled the scandalous waltz, it was lavishly praised in 1850 by London's *Punch*: "La Polka, as danced in Paris and now adopted by us, is elegant, graceful, and fascinating in the extreme. It is replete with opportunities of showing care and attention to your partner in assisting her through its performance." Into the early 20th century, copulation was occasionally referred to as the "matrimonial polka."

awblaster

A cross-bowman.

—John Jamieson's *Etymological Dictionary of the Scottish Language*, 1808

Toxophilite, a lover or devotee of archery.

—Sir James Murray's *New English Dictionary*, 1926

From Weapon to Sport

Peter Ditchfield's *Old English Sports, Pastimes and Customs* (1891) examined the history of archery in England, which declined into Victorian times, except in women's "toxophilite" (see above) associations: "Edward III ordered 'that everyone strong in body, at leisure on holidays, should use in their recreation bows and arrows and learn and exercise the art of shooting, forsaking such vain plays as throwing stones, handball, bandyball, or cockfighting, which have no profit in them.' Edward IV ordered every Englishman, of whatever rank, to have a bow his own height always ready for use, and to instruct his children in the art. In every township [including London's district, Newington Butts, named for its targets] the butts were ordered to be set up, and the people were required to shoot 'up and down' every Sunday and feast day, under penalty of one halfpenny. The sport began to decline in the 16th century in spite of royal proclamations and occasional revivals."

sniggling

A peculiar mode of catching eels in small streams and ponds, described by Izaak Walton [see below].

—Admiral William Smyth's Sailor's Word-Book, 1867

Take a strong, small hook, tied to a string about a yard long, and then into the hole where an eel may hide himself, with a short stick put in a bait leisurely. If within the sight of it, an eel will bite. Pull him out by degrees.

—Richard Coxe's Pronouncing Dictionary, 1813

Fishing for a Good Disposition

Izaak Walton (1593–1683) promoted the concept of the true gentleman in his book, *The Compleat Angler, or Contemplative Man's Recreation* (1653). It proved so popular that it has been reprinted more than one hundred times, and even in America many fishing clubs have been named after Walton. He urged reader-fishermen to approach angling with respect, suggesting that the living creature be handled with care when securing it to a line, "using him as though you loved him; that is, harm him as little as you may possibl[y], that he may live the

 longer." Long before the Animal Rights movement, this book helped civilize fishermen. It received critical acclaim by readers such as Charles Lamb, who observed, "It might sweeten a man's temper at any time to read *The Compleat Angler*." In it, Walton wrote, "I love such mirth as does not make friends ashamed to look upon one another next morning."

canvas opera

A circus.

—Maurice Weseen's *Dictionary of American Slang*, 1934

Circus Free-for-All

English circus purveyor "Lord" George Sanger described a bizarre confrontation among traveling rival performers in his autobiography, *Seventy Years a Showman* (1910). In 1833, "about two miles from Reading [Berkshire], on the Oxford road," Sanger witnessed a brawl between Hilton's and Wombwell's competing carnivals. He reported, "Even the freaks took part. The fat man made for the living skeleton with a door-hook; the living skeleton battered at the fat man with a peg mallet. Windows and doors of caravans were smashed. . . . While the mêlée was at its height there came a terrible diversion. The horses drawing Wombwell's elephants, left unattended, had taken fright at the noise made by the fighting, swearing men and wild beasts who, aroused by the combat, added their howling to the din. In two minutes the elephants, mad with fright, had smashed the sides of the wagon to splinters, and made their way out, rushing hither and thither, and turning over everything in their path."

In the end, no lives were lost, but the turmoil was never forgotten — at least not by the participants.

gleek

A joke; a jeer; a scoff. In some of the notes on this word it has been supposed to be connected with the card-game of gleek; but it was not recollected that the Saxon language supplied the term *glig* and doubtless a corresponding verb. Thus *glee* signifies mirth and jocularity; and *gleeman* or *gligman*, a minstrel or joculator. Gleek was therefore used to express a stronger sort of joke, a scoffing. It does not appear that the phrase *to give the gleek* was ever introduced in the above game, which was borrowed by us from the French, and derived from an original of very different import from the word in question. . . . *To give the minstrel* is no more than a punning phrase for giving the gleek. Minstrels and jesters were anciently called *gleekmen* or *gligmen*.

—Rev. Alexander Dyce's *Glossary to the Works of Shakespeare*, 1902

Another Use for Playing Cards

Madame Celnart's *Gentleman and Lady's Book of Politeness and*

Propriety of Deportment (1855) described the makings of early business cards from recycled paper: "It was not considered impolite formerly to take the cards of a cast off pack [of playing cards], cut them crosswise into three parts, and write one's name upon them. This, however, is now a subject of ridicule, and is only seen in provincial towns."

divoteer

A golfer.

—Sydney Baker's *A Popular Dictionary of Australian Slang*, 1943

Fore!

Forerunners of this game probably date back to Roman "pagenica," in which leather balls were hit into holes with curved wooden sticks. "Kolf" was also played in Holland in the town of Loenen aan de Vecht in 1297, according to one written record. In this one-hole affair, the winner was whoever could hit a leather ball into a hole a hundred yards away with the fewest strokes. Another Dutch contest about that time involved hitting a ball into a hole in a frozen lake. Many old paintings depict early golfers, but few written records have been found.

In 1754, twenty-two "Noblemen and Gentlemen" contributed to a silver club to be played for annually at famous St. Andrew's in Scotland. The competition was initially open to all, as it had been in 1744 for the golfers of Leith, whose rules St. Andrew's golfers adopted with only minor changes. But the earliest records of golf in Scotland date from 1457, when King James II proclaimed that the game be "utterley cryed down" because it interfered with his troops' archery practice.

Etiquette, Fashion and Folly

Etiquette is the barrier which society draws around itself as a protection against offences the law cannot touch. It is a shield against the impertinent, the improper, and the vulgar — a guard against those obtuse persons who, having neither talent nor delicacy, would be continually thrusting themselves into the society of men to whom their presence might be offensive.

—Charles William Day's *Hints on Etiquette and the Uses of Society, With a Glance at Bad Habits,* 1834

tailor's mense

A small portion left by way of good manners. In some parts of the North it is the custom for the village tailor to work at his customer's house, and to partake of the hospitality of the family board. On these occasions the best fare is invariably provided; at least such was the case when I was a boy; and the tailor to shew that he has had enough, generally leaves a little on his plate, which is called *tailor's mense*. [From] *mense*, decency, propriety of conduct, good manners, kindness, hospitality.

—John Brockett's *Glossary of North Country Words*, 1825

Menseful, neat; mannerly; proper; well-behaved; well-dressed.

—Francis Taylor's *The Folk-Speech of South Lancashire*, 1901

Take That Last Morsel

In *The Young Man's Companion* (1866) Edward Turner recommended against the tailor's mense: "Avoid that most vulgar habit which prevails among half-bred country people of abstaining from taking the last piece on a dish. It amounts almost to an insult towards your host to do anything which shows that you fear that the vacancy cannot be supplied and that there is likely to be a scarcity.... Rather go out of your way and make a point of taking the last piece than do anything which indicates that you hold such an opinion."

cockstride

The length of a cock's stride. "The days are getting a *cockstride* longer."

—Thomas Darlington's *The Folk-Speech of South Cheshire*, 1887

I'm Late, I'm Late ...

When Henry VIII disbanded Britain's churches and monasteries in 1540, London's Covent Garden was seized and developed into a secular district, including the famous Covent Garden Theatre. The custom of being "fashionably late" arose there and in similar venues, according to the anonymous American book of etiquette, *Manners That Win, Compiled from the Latest Authorities* (1884): "Our practice of arriving late doubtless grew out of the habits of the English. There, a gentleman or lady of rank may have several engagements in a single evening — going from dinner to opera, and from opera to several balls. In England, therefore, a late arrival might mean that the necessities of these social demands were so great that an earlier arrival was impossible — an indication of social importance. In America, where no such meaning could attach to it, the adoption of such a custom is absurd, especially when it is a great inconvenience to men who are not gentlemen of leisure like the English aristocrats but men of business who need plenty of rest. If we must copy customs from abroad, let us discriminate between those suited to our mode of life and those which were meant for an entirely different state of things."

dontles

Clothes, articles to be donned; hence *donetlement*, holiday dress, fine clothes. Lancashire. *Holiday-jack*, a man fond of holidays and the display of clothes.

—Joseph Wright's *English Dialect Dictionary*, 1898–1905

Vacation Etiquette — First Calls

When summer drew near, vacationers going to countryside retreats once considered these complex Victorian "rules of first calls" from Henrietta Ward's *Sensible Etiquette from the Best Society* (1878): "At watering-places and country estates, calls are made upon those who arrive later. At places of summer resort, those who own their cottages call upon each other according to the priority of arrival, while both those who own and who rent call first upon friends arriving at hotels. In first calls, it is well to remember the 'English rule' — the lady of the highest rank makes the first call. When it becomes a question as to which shall call first between persons occupying neighbouring

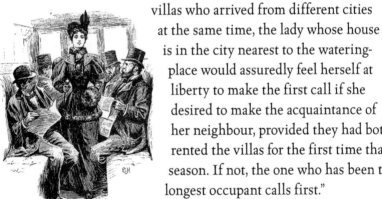

villas who arrived from different cities at the same time, the lady whose house is in the city nearest to the watering-place would assuredly feel herself at liberty to make the first call if she desired to make the acquaintance of her neighbour, provided they had both rented the villas for the first time that season. If not, the one who has been the longest occupant calls first."

fucate

To paint, disguise, colour, or counterfeit a thing by making it look abundantly more beautiful than it really is.

—Thomas Dyche's *General English Dictionary*, 1740

Kiss and Make Up

In 1667, London chronicler John Evelyn noted women's make-up fashions, writing, "I now observed how the women began to paint themselves, formerly a most ignominious thing and us'd only by prostitutes." Decades earlier, Elizabeth I had attempted to discourage women from "tricking" men into marriage with make-up, false hair, padding, heels, and hips, although she whitened her own face and plucked her forehead.

Even a century ago, T. F. Thiselton-Dyer's *Folklore of Women* (1905) pointed out the use of "facial paint," writing caustically: "A proverb which, under a variety of forms, is found in our own and other countries, runs 'Let no woman's painting breed thy heart's fainting.' . . . A practice of rouging has . . . from a very early period, been a recognised emblem of a 'fast' woman, and an Italian adage runs 'women rouge that they may not blush.' Hence we are told that 'a woman who paints puts up a bill [which reads] *to let*,' with which we may compare the popular adage, 'a woman and a cherry are painted for their own harm.'" Later, Thiselton-Dyer warned against selecting "a jewel, a woman, or linen by candlelight — by candlelight, a goat looks like a lady."

codpiece

A part of the male dress, formerly made very conspicuous.

—Robert Nares's *Glossary of the Works of English Authors*, 1859

Consider the Codpiece

The triangular British codpiece, which looked something like an ornate, oversized jockstrap, was once used to proclaim and exaggerate the male genitalia. This curious pronouncement of virility was sported by the likes of Henry VIII, who added one to his suit of armor, now on display at Windsor Castle. It was believed to bring fertility to barren women who touched it with a pin. Even Henry's nine-year-old son, soon-to-be-king Edward VI, can be seen wearing one in portraiture.

Cod was a synonym for bag and, by extension, the scrotum. Conceived in the late 1400s, this clothing accessory was worn by European aristocrats, and known to the French as the boastful-sounding *braguette.* The padding and animal-bone framework eventually increased to ridiculous proportions, giving the wearer the appearance of permanent sexual arousal. This bizarre fashion accessory reached the height of its popularity by the 1560s, being studded with gemstones, precious metals, and feathers, and used occasionally to support flagpoles in marching processions. After then it shrank and was considered a "style of Venetians."

buttermilk cow

A bull. When children ask why a bull is not milked, they are told that he is a "buttermilk cow."

—Rollo Brown's *Word List from Western Indiana*, 1912

Inexpressibles, a euphemism for trousers.

—Richard Thornton's *American Glossary*, 1912

Write No Evil?

In 1704, America's first continuously-published newspaper, the *Boston News-Letter*, printed its first issue. Sounding a bit prudish, French visitor Maria Theresa Longworth had little good to say about the American newspapers she read 170 years later in her book *Teresina in America* (1875): "American newspapers contain most startling reading to strangers unaccustomed to such exposés. In England or France they would soon be suppressed by law. Their effect on young minds must be most destructive to all purity and innocence. I was informed that an Act of Congress was in progress to restrain this wholesale exposure of vice. Notwithstanding all this, ladies pretend to faint if they hear the words 'bull' or 'donkey.' There are houses, certainly, where newspapers are not admitted into the family.... American ladies display their legs as do Boulogne *matelottes* [risqué women from Paris's Bois de Boulogne] but to mention them greatly shocks their sensibilities. They are particular even to straitlacedness in what they say, but not often in what they do."

sumptify

To be at great expense.

—Elisha Coles's *An English Dictionary*, 1713

Making the Best of Sumptuary Laws

Influential Scottish political economist Adam Smith (1723-1790) addressed the subject of England's "sumptuary laws" — an arbitrary control of conspicuous consumption which forbade the indulgence in certain luxuries by commoners. *Blackstone's Law Commentaries* (1765–1769) cautioned, for example, "that no man shall be served more than two courses, except in some great holiday, therein specified, on which he shall be served with three." In his economics classic *The Wealth of Nations* (1776), Smith wrote, "It is the highest impertinence and presumption in kings and ministers to pretend to watch over the economy of private people and to restrain their expense — either by sumptuary laws or by prohibiting the importation of foreign luxuries. They are themselves always, and without any exception, the greatest spendthrifts in the society."

Many of these statutes, enacted between the 1300s and 1600s, remained in effect into Victorian times, such as one reflected in E. B. Duffey's *Ladies' and Gentlemen's Etiquette* (1877), "A rich man may be forgiven for wearing a threadbare coat, but a poor man is inexcusable for appearing in fine broadcloth and dressing his wife and daughters in silks, velvets, and diamonds."

upper ten

Of the common sort; ordinary; [related to *gregarious*] belonging to a herd.

—William Grimshaw's *Ladies' Lexicon and Parlour Companion*, 1854

Gregarianism, the practice of collecting in flocks or companies.

—Sir James Murray's *New English Dictionary*, 1901

Lord Chesterfield Meant Well

Philip Stanhope (shown here), the overbearing 4th Earl of Chesterfield, warned his illegitimate adult son Philip against indulging in forms of low-life behavior, such as using "folk-speech." In a letter dated 1741, he cautioned: "There is an awkwardness of expression and words most carefully to be avoided, such as false English, bad pronunciation, old sayings, and common proverbs, which are so many proofs of having kept bad company. For example, if instead of saying that tastes are different, and that every man has his own peculiar one, you should [offer] a proverb and say that 'What is one man's meat is another man's poison,' or else, 'Everyone as they like, as the good man said when he kissed the cow,' everybody would be persuaded that you had never kept company with anybody above footmen and housemaids."

Nine years later, after causing his son to wed secretly against his wishes, the elder Stanhope concluded a correspondence by admitting, "I wish to God you had as much pleasure in following my advice as I have in giving it to you."

Etiquette, Fashion and Folly

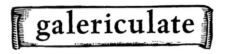

galericulate

Covered, as with a hat.
—Samuel Johnson's *Dictionary of the English Language*, 1755

The Top-Hat Riot

The classic top-hat design is usually attributed to Middlesex tailor George Dunnage, and depictions of earlier hats can be dated to 1747. But in 1797, another top-hat designer, London Strand clothier John Hetherington debuted his creation by riding about town in a carriage. According to legend, the public's alarmed reaction was unexpected, with groups of pedestrians gathering to loudly voice their disapproval. Hetherington was arrested, forced to post an enormous £500 bond, and brought before the Lord Mayor, who fined him £50. The prosecutor charged that he had "appeared upon the public highway wearing upon his head what he called a 'silk hat' . . . calculated to frighten timid people," and that "several women fainted at the unusual sight, while children screamed, dogs yelped, and a younger son of Cordwainer Thomas . . . was thrown down by the crowd . . . and had his right arm broken." But this hat, originally made of beaver, was only a reworked version of a riding hat with a lower crown and wider brim made from beaver pelts. The top hat caught on slowly, although a French magician named Louis Comte gladly became the first conjurer to publicly pull a rabbit from one in 1814. Worldwide popularity would wait until 1850, when Prince Albert began wearing top hats.

The Best of Forgotten English

bone-orchard

A slang name for a cemetery.

—Ramon Adams's *Western Words: A Dictionary of the Range, Cow Camps, and Trail,* 1946

Long-home, the grave.

—Charles Mackay's *Lost Beauties of the English Language,* 1874

Sprucing Up Boston's Cemeteries

Alice Morse Earle's *Customs and Fashions in Old New England* (1893) described a disingenuous tidying of Boston's graveyards, a practice that occurred in many places in America. "Early graves were frequently clustered, [and] were even crowded in irregular groups in the churchyard. . . . In the first half of this century, a precise superintendent of graveyards and his army of assistants . . . straightened out mathematically all the old burial-places, levelled the earth, and set in trim military rows the old slate headstones, regardless of the irregular clusters of graves and their occupants. And there in Boston, the falsifying old headstones still stand, fixed in new places, but marking no coffins or honored bones beneath — the only true words of their inscriptions being the opening ones, *Here lies.*"

purseproud

Puffed up with riches.

—William Scott's *Dictionary of the English Language*, 1791

Thinking highly of one's self on account of wealth.

—Richard Coxe's *Pronouncing Dictionary*, 1813

Yabblement, strong, able. A *yabbish* lot, people of wealth.

—Margaret Ann Courtnay's *Glossary of Words
in Use in West Cornwall*, 1880

The Great Pretense

The anonymous *Gentleman's Hand-Book of Etiquette and Guide to Polite Society* (1860) recommended that a man, when visiting the rich and powerful, "never praise, nor even look at, the pictures, the carpets, the curtains, or the ottomans because if he did it might be supposed that he was not accustomed to such things." Beyond this, "a man of fashion must never allow himself to be pleased. Nothing is more decidedly *de mauvais ton* than any expression of delight. He must never laugh, nor . . . even smile, for he might, by ignorance, smile at the wrong place or time. All real emotion is to be avoided; all sympathy with the great or beautiful is to be shunned."

In *Walden* (1854), American philosopher Henry David Thoreau addressed the subject of luxuries metaphysically, remarking, "A man is rich in proportion to the number of things which he can afford to leave alone."

sub-blush

To blush slightly.

—Edward Lloyd's *Encyclopædic Dictionary*, 1895

Introducing Rev. Thomas Bowdler (1754–1825)

Sanitized synonyms, still known as *bowdlerisms* (related to the verb *bowdlerize*, "to emasculate through squeamishness") were found in Bowdler's best-selling 1818 edition of the Bard's works, as well as his editions of such works as the Old Testament and Edward Gibbon's *Decline and Fall of the Roman Empire*. His ten-volume Shakespeare avoided anything "which cannot with propriety be read aloud in a family," such as Lady Macbeth's admonishment, "Out, damn'd spot!" — which was purified to read "Out, *crimson* spot!" Bowdler, who had abandoned a medical career three decades earlier because patients made him "queasy," explained that he wished to present this material without "anything that could raise a blush on the cheek of modesty."

Queen Victoria (shown here beside Albert) — who until age 18 was not allowed to read popular books or even walk outdoors or on stairs unattended — was likely a fan of Bowdler. She wrote to her daughter, Victoria, in 1859: "By the by, you went to see the *Merry Wives*. I have never had the courage to go to see it — having always been told how very coarse it was — for your adored Shakespeare is dreadful in that respect, and many things have to be left out in many plays."

peelaflee

A light person, and not heavily clothed.

—John Mactaggart's *Scottish Gallovidian Encyclopedia*, 1824

From the idea of stripping a fly of its covering.

—John Jamieson's *Etymological Dictionary of the Scottish Language*, 1808

Unray, to divest of clothes; to undress, strip.

—Sir James Murray's *New English Dictionary*, 1926

Undoff, to undress.

—Thomas Wright's *Dictionary of Obsolete and Provincial English*, 1857

French Origins of the Striptease

In 1893, the earliest documented striptease was performed at the Bal des Quatre Arts, held at Paris's notorious Moulin Rouge. This groundbreaking but subtle bump-and-grind was enacted by a woman remembered simply as Mona, who normally earned at least a portion of her living by posing nude for painters and sculptors. About a year later, the first professional peep show, known as "Le Coucher d'Yvette" — X-rated by 19th-century standards, but undoubtedly very tame by today's — began at the nearby Fayonau Music Hall. In that fleeting display of flesh, Yvette attracted voyeuristic audiences by portraying a woman who disrobed before going to bed. Soon afterward, local imitators titillated patrons of burlesque entertainment by developing knockoff routines based on other domestic activities, such as bathing.

bienseance

Decorum; propriety. Rather common in English use about the end of the 18th and [the] beginning of [the] 19th centuries. From French *bien*, well, and *séant*, past participle of [French] *seoir*, to befit. . . . *Etiquettical*, pertaining to etiquette.

—Sir James Murray's *New English Dictionary*, 1888

Belluine, beastly, brutal.

—John Boag's *Imperial Lexicon of the English Language*, c. 1850

To Slouch or Not to Slouch?

An anonymous book of etiquette, *The American Chesterfield* (1828), reported on a common impropriety among lawyers and in church: "There is another habit peculiar to the United States, and from which some females who call themselves 'ladies' are not free — that of lolling back, balanced upon the two hind legs of a chair. Such a breach of good breeding is rarely committed in Europe. Lolling is carried even so far in America that it is not uncommon to see attorneys lay their feet upon the council table, and the clerks and judges theirs also upon their desks in open court. But low-bred and disgusting as is this practice in a court of justice, how much more reprehensible is it in places of still greater solemnity of character. How must the feelings of a truly religious man be wounded when he sees the legs extended in the same indecent posture in the House of God!"

Food, Dining and Cookery

The most disagreeable thing at sea is the cookery, for there is not, properly speaking, any professional cook on board. The worst sailor is generally chosen for that purpose. Hence comes the proverb used among English sailors, "God sends meat, but the devil sends cooks."

—Benjamin Franklin's essay, *Precautions to be Used by Those Who are About to Undertake Sea Voyages*, 1793

jamrags

Anything overcooked.

—J. H. Nodal's *Glossary of the Lancashire Dialect*, 1882

Forslockened, overdone.

—Thomas Wright's *Dictionary of Obsolete and Provincial English*, 1857

A French Look at American Meals

While visiting New England, French traveler Maria Theresa Longworth noted some New World dining habits, which she included in *Teresina in America* (1875): "An American dinner, so called, is a curiosity of indigestion, so much that the Americans have nearly always to retire to their beds after eating it, and bear unmistakable tokens of it in their sallow, lean persons. The manner of serving it, and the multiplicity of bits and scraps, resembles more the Turkish style of dinner than anything I know in Europe. You are served with one plate, knife, and fork, and around are placed from one to two more score of small dishes or saucers resembling those in a child's toy dinner set. In each dish there is a bit of something — a spoonful of turnip, a boiled potato, ditto mashed, a sweet potato, a parsnip, onions raw, cold cabbage, and warm sauerkraut and celery — in short, an endless variety of vegetables. The fish, flesh, and fowl are as badly cooked. It requires frequently a good deal of discrimination to distinguish beef from veal, pork from mutton."

The Best of Forgotten English

make a long arm

To reach far, especially when trying to help oneself to food.

—J. C. Ruppenthal's *Word-List from Kansas*, 1916

Language of the Greasy Spoon

In 1872, Providence, Rhode Island, newsman Walter Scott began operating America's first horse-drawn food dispensary. From this humble beginning, the American diner was born. The French word *café* gave rise to *cafeteria*, which in turn spawned such silly and discarded shop names as *groceteria*, *caketeria*, *furnitureteria*, *candyteria*, *smoketeria*, *shaveteria*, *garmenteria*, *drugeteria*, and even *casketeria*.

The café developed a unique vocabulary, with such colorful terms as *Adam and Eve on a raft* for two eggs on toast, and its variant, *wrecked Adam and Eve* for scrambled eggs. *One-two-three-and-a-splash* was understood by short-order cooks and servers as a dish of meat, potato, bread, and gravy, and *one foot in the grave* requested an order of soup, since invalids often ate it, while *zepplin in a hanger* got the customer a bunned frankfurter. A glass of tap water was *one on the city*, or a *tin roof* (because it's "on the house"), and *Missouri River* specified gravy, playing on that river's nickname, *Big Muddy*. Other terms bandied about in diners included *first lady* for spareribs (referring to Eve); *Bossie in a bowl*, beef stew; *cat's beer*, milk; *whistleberries*, beans; and *clean the kitchen*, hash.

forty gallons of soup

The great blue heron has been fabled "forty gallons of soup" for its strong flavor.

—Frederic Cassidy's *Dictionary of American Regional English*, 1991

Fashionable Feasting on Fowl

In pre-industrial Britain, a wide variety of wild birds was consumed, including seagulls, vultures, and even small songbirds, and specific verbs were employed for speaking about carving some of them. In his [Medical] *Receipts* (1696), William Salmon offered these examples: "*rear* that goose; *fract* that chicken; *sauce* that capon; *unbrace* that mallard; *dismember* that heron; *disfigure* that peacock; *display* that crane; *untach* that curlew; *unjoin* that bittern; *allay* that pheasant; *wing* that quail; *mince* that plover."

The anonymous book, *The Perfect Gentleman, or Etiquette and Eloquence* (1860), also helped readers enlarge their vocabularies when serving fowl: "In the 17th century, carving was a science that carried with it as much pedantry as schoolteaching does at present, and for a person to use wrong terms in relation to carving was an unpardonable affront to etiquette. Carving all kinds of small birds

was called to *thy* them; a pheasant, to *allay* it; a duck, to *embrace* it; a hen, to *spoil* her; a goose, to *tare* her, and a list of similar technicalities too ridiculous to repeat." Samuel Johnson advised, "You should praise, not ridicule, your friend who carves with as much earnestness of purpose as though he were legislating." The 16th-century woman at left is serving a cooked peacock.

quail-mutton

The flesh of sheep that have died of disease, from drowning, or natural causes. From Anglo-Saxon *cwelan*, to die.

—R. E. G. Cole's *Words Used in Southwest Lincolnshire*, 1886

Making the Most of Meat

John Mactaggart's *Scottish Gallovidian Encyclopedia* (1824) described meat called "braxy-hams": "The hams of those sheep which die of the braxy ['splenic apoplexy']. When the [shep]herd finds any of his flock dead of that distemper, if they can stand three shakes — that is to say, if they be not so putrified or rotten that they can stand to be thrice shaken by the neck without falling to pieces — then he bears them home. . . . Carcasses can then be ham'd, and the rest of the flesh made present use of. *Braxy* is by no means bad food when ham'd; the smell in a great measure leaves it. These hams sometimes adorn the saddle-bow of a moorland lover when he starts on horseback to seek a wife, and are considered to aid him much . . . with any girl he takes a fancy for."

In America, well-decayed lamb was known as "bob veal" and sold in "secondhand food markets." Wool called *mortlings* or *pluck-wool* was that taken from dead English sheep, and mutton from sheep which died a natural death was referred to as "hump-gutteral." John Hotten's *Slang Dictionary* (1887) mentioned "an animal to whom the knife only just anticipated death from natural disease or accident; said of meat on that account unfit for human food."

graillon

A dirty, slatternly woman — one who emits an odour of kitchen grease.

—Albert Barrère's *French and English Dictionary: Cant Words, Quaint Expressions and Flash Phrases Used in High and Low Life*, 1889

Alternative Cuisine

In the summer of 1870, the Franco-Prussian War officially began. By September 20, the Prussian army had unexpectedly sealed off the French capital, and Parisians were forced to think creatively about meals for the next four months. During that time, butchers sold the meat of more than 500 horses per day, more "cheval" than had ever been consumed before. As protein sources dwindled, dogs and cats began disappearing from the streets and reappearing on middle-class Parisian dinner tables. A special market for the plumpest rats was even established, and brave residents began creating palatable recipes for these delicacies.

The newspaper *Les Nouvelles* suggested such questionable dishes as rat stew, dog chops with peas, sliced saddle of cat, dog liver kebabs, horse soup with millet, and cat stew with mushrooms. Sadly, the zoo was forced to sell hungry consumers the larger animals it could not feed, including zebras, yaks, two elephants, and a hippo. Stranded in Paris, British MP Henry Labouchère reported that mouflon, a tough Corsican "goat-antelope," was among the available zoo "luxuries." But he noted dryly, "I do not think that I shall take up my residence in Corsica in order to habitually feed upon it."

thumb-bucka

A thick slice of bread on which butter is spread with the thumb.

—Sidney Addy's *Glossary of Words used in the Neighbourhood of Sheffield,* 1888

Renaissance Health Tips

Physician to Henry VIII, Andrew Boorde (c. 1490–1549) advised his readers of a stress reduction technique: "In your garden dig one or two large pools, and stock them with carp. . . . Sitting by the pool on a warm day and watching the fish is a most pleasant way of calming the mind."

In his *Dyetary of Health* (1542) Boorde wrote about bread: "Bread made of wheat maketh a man fat, especially when the bread is made of new wheat. Evil bakers will put wheat and barley together. Bread made of these aforesaid corns may fill the gut, but shall never do good to man, no more than bread made of beans and pease will do. Hot bread is unwholesome to any man, for it doth lie in the stomach like a sponge, yet the smell of new bread is comfortable to the head and heart. Old or stale bread doth dry up the blood, or natural moisture in man, and doth engender ill humours, and is evil and tardy of digestion; wherefore is no surfeit so evil as the surfeit of eating naughty [unwholesome] bread." Even as late as 1868, Henry Lunettes agreed, cautioning in *The American Gentleman's Guide to Politeness and Fashion,* "Warm bread, as a rule, is unsuited to the human stomach."

plaw

A slight boiling. If meat seems likely to be tainted before it can be dressed, the cook must "give it a plaw" to check the progress of decay. It may be from some French term of cookery, in books not easily accessible, or from Anglo-Saxon *pleoh*, [danger].

—Rev. Robert Forby's *Vocabulary of East Anglia*, 1830

The Perfect Cook

In his *English Housewife* (1615), Gervase Markham wrote, "The cook must be cleanly both in body and garments. She must have a quick eye, a curious nose, a perfect taste, and a ready ear, and she must not be butter-fingered, sweet-toothed, nor faint-hearted. For the first will let everything fall, the second will consume what it should increase, and the last will lose time with too much niceness."

Elsewhere, Markham listed the mythical servant's "general virtues," stating, "Our English housewife must be of chaste thought, stout courage, patient, untired, watchful, diligent, witty, pleasant, constant in friendship, full of good neighbourhood, wise in discourse but not frequent therein, sharp and quick of speech, but not bitter or talkative, secret in her affairs, comfortable in her counsels, and generally skillful in all worthy knowledges which do belong to her vocation."

traveling-couvert

A set of table utensils, knife, fork, spoon and drinking-cup, made to pack closely for use in traveling. The longer articles were sometimes made to separate into two parts, or with hinges by which they could be closed together for packing.

—William Whitney's *Century Dictionary*, 1889

The Fork Arrives in England

Thomas Coryate (c. 1577–1617), considered the first Englishman to have used a fork (a two-pronged variety), walked to India and died there of dysentery on about this date. At home, he was ridiculed as effeminate for his pioneering table manners. In *Coryat's Crudities: Hastily Gobbled Up in Five Months Travels in France, Savoy, Italy, &c.* (1611), he described the early use of utensils: "I observed a custome in those Italian cities and townes through which I passed. The Italian, and also most strangers that are commorant in Italy, doe alwaies at their meales use a little forke when they cut meate. In the company of others at meate, should [one] unadvisedly touch the dish of meate with his fingers, from which all at the table doe cut, he will give offence as having transgressed the lawes of good manners. For his error he shall be at least browbeaten, if not reprehended in words."

By mid-Victorian times, tableware had become an English obsession, and one manufacturer offered over 140 pieces of a particular pattern in its catalog. English aristocrats and monarchs as late as Queen Anne often used their hands for consuming roast chicken.

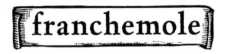

franchemole

A dish in ancient cookery composed chiefly of eggs and sheep's fat.

—James Halliwell's *Dictionary of Archaic and Provincial Words*, 1855

The Medicinal Cooking of Kenelm Digby

His writings, such as *The Closet of Sir Kenelm Digby Opened* (1669), linked English cooking to medicine through strange recipes like "Hart's-horn gelly." The first hundred pages of his *Closet* were devoted to recipes for dozens of liquors such as metheglins, meaths, ciders, bragots, sack-possets, syllabubs and aqua vitae, some of which were made with "conduit water" and "whipped with a birchen-rod."

Although he was ridiculed for his use of outdated principles of alchemy, this anonymous epitaph (with a mistaken birth date) reveals the respect he garnered from contemporaries:

Born on the day he died, the eleventh of June,
And that day bravely fought at Scandaroon;
It's rare that one and the same day should be
His day of birth, of death, and victory!

Digby (shown here) was hailed for healing a friend's stab-wound, suffered when that friend tried unsuccessfully to part two duelers. Digby treated the bandages that had bound the wound, from which the patient reported experiencing a placebo effect, feeling a "pleasing kind of freshnesse, as if it were a wet, cold napkin spread over my hand."

abliguration

A prodigal spending on meat and drink.

—Samuel Johnson's *Dictionary of the English Language*, 1755

Dropping Pounds With William Banting

a London undertaker and cabinetmaker who developed a successful weight-loss program. In 1863, he published a pamphlet describing how he had shed 46 pounds and 12 inches of girth due to his abstention from almost everything except meat. Preferring to lace up the corset rather than alter their food intake, Victorians eagerly read Banting's writings, yet few practiced his techniques. But they were influenced enough to begin using the terms "to bant" and "doing banting" when they referred to dieting. Inspired by Banting's pamphlet, H. S. Leigh's *Carols of Cockayne* (1869) included:

> If you wish to grow thinner, diminish your dinner,
> And take to light claret instead of pale ale;
> Look down with an utter contempt upon butter,
> And never touch bread till it's toasted or stale.

Into the 17th century, vegetables were avoided by the English upper classes for their supposed tendency to generate flatulence and melancholy. And root crops such as carrots and turnips were suspected of having links to the devil, and raw fruit was widely considered "peasant food" and a source of various maladies.

wild fowl flavor

Tasty and appetizing food was said to have a real "wild fowl flavor." The dish in question might be a pie or any kind of food. Nantucket.

—William Macy's *The Nantucket Scrap Basket*, 1930

A Few Restaurant Tidbits

The origins of the word "restaurant" may be found in what has been considered the world's second oldest restaurant. In 1765, a Monsieur Boulanger is believed to have opened a Paris eatery that served only sheep's feet simmered in a white sauce, which he claimed was a health "restorative" — from the French verb *restaurer*, to restore. He displayed a sign informing passersby that "Boulanger sells magic restoratives." Until the chef hung out his claim, a Parisian guild had enjoyed a monopoly on prepared foods, which its members sold to the taverns where the food was served and consumed, and its members sued Boulanger for infringement on their exclusive right to offer cooked edibles. But he was vindicated by the court in

a ruling that opened the door for countless restaurants across Paris, which numbered about 500 by 1804. The term "restaurant" and the dining concept were adopted throughout Europe, and were eventually found worldwide. But Stockholm's Den Gyldene Freden, begun in 1722, is considered the oldest, and is still serving wonderful meals.

compiss

To wet with urine; adaptation of French *compisser*.

—Sir James Murray's *New English Dictionary*, 1893

Before the Water Closet

Renowned English cabinetmaker Thomas Chippendale was born in Otley, West Yorkshire. His creations included many formal dining-room tables and chairs, desks and a number of curious accessories. A once-popular but largely forgotten bedroom convenience he designed was innocuously called the "night table." This narrow, waist-high, four-legged cabinet featured a top that hinged upward and two doors that opened forward, revealing an elegant chamber pot.

Before the advent of indoor plumbing, chamber pots were also concealed in cabinetry by Chippendale's successors, such as one installed in the library at Flintham Hall, near Newark, Nottinghamshire. In 1784, after visiting a family at Norfolk's Houghton Hall, whose dining room was furnished with such a screened piece of easement furniture for men, Frenchman François de la Rochefoucauld reported disdainfully,

"The sideboard is garnished also with chamber pots in keeping with the common practice of going over to the sideboard to pee while the others are drinking. Nothing is hidden. I find that very indecent." But in fact the French sometimes employed the same sort of device, which was used by women as well.

buckard

Milk, soured by keeping too long in the bucket, or by being kept in a foul bucket. The word is not now used, but is applied to cheese when instead of being solid it has a spongy look and is full of cavities.

—Frederick Elworthy's *Specimens of English Dialects*, 1879

Muckered, said of milk that has acquired a bad flavour, but not become sour.

—Georgina Jackson's *Shropshire Word-Book*, 1879

Hold the Mayo

In 1762 the first formally acknowledged "sandwich" since Roman times — made from slices of beef and cheese, spiced, and served between slices of toasted bread — was devised for John Montagu, 4th Earl of Sandwich and First Lord of the Admiralty. As a gambling addict, Montagu could spend twenty-four uninterrupted hours at the gaming tables and needed a convenient form of sustenance that left one hand free for dice and cards.

Despite the name they shared, it seems that Montagu's ancestor Edward, 1st Earl of Sandwich, had only the slightest relationship

with the town of Sandwich. In fact, he had intended to take the title of 1st Earl of Portsmouth, but one day in 1660 a group of ships he was commanding happened to anchor off Sandwich, and he simply decided to flatter the town's citizens by drawing his moniker from their home. So, had his choice been otherwise, today's "sandwich" might have been called a "portsmouth" instead.

drink-meat

Ale, boiled, thickened with oatmeal, and spiced. [Also *spoon-meat*.]

—Georgina Jackson's *Shropshire Word-Book*, 1879

Meat-earth, cultivated land. Devonshire.

—James Halliwell's *Dictionary of Archaic and Provincial Words*, 1855

The Many Kinds of Meat

Just as *liquor* once indicated any liquid, *meat* described a variety of edibles over the last thousand years. Edward Lloyd's 1895 dictionary defined *meat* this way: "Originally, food of all kinds. *Horse-meat* is still used locally for fodder, and *green-meat* is often applied to edible vegetables, such as lettuces." In 1775, Samuel Johnson wrote in his *Journey to the Western Islands of Scotland*: "The horses could not travel all day without rest or meat." From the 1400s to the 1800s, *whitemeat* — now the lighter meat of fowls, and the flesh of lamb, veal, and rabbit in Britain — indicated "food made of milk," as per Samuel Johnson's 1755 dictionary. Berries were once known as "birds'-meat," and into modern times, butter and cheese have been known as *milkmeats*, candies are *sweetmeats*, and the edible part of *fruit* is dubbed "flesh."

Mercutio referred to meat twice in *Romeo and Juliet*, first telling Benvolio, "Thy head is as full of quarrels as an egg is full of *meat*." Later, as he lay mortally wounded, he shouted, "They have made worm's *meat* of me!" A well known proverb originally stated, "One man's *meat* is another's poison."

verjuice

A kind of harsh vinegar made of the expressed juice of the wild apple or crab [apple] which has undergone acetous fermentation.

—Richard Hoblyn's *Medical Dictionary*, 1859

An acid liquor prepared from very sour grapes or crabapples.

—Robley Dunglison's *Dictionary of Medical Science*, 1844

From French *verd*, green, and *jus*, juice; used in sauces . . . and the like.

—T. Ellwood Zell's *Encyclopedia of Knowledge and Language*, 1871

What was Verjuice?

Verjuice, which was succeeded in southern Europe by the introduction of the New World tomato, had largely lost its place on the cook's shelf by the early 1800s, but it remained in metaphorical use to describe an unpleasant disposition, as in Theodore Hook's *The Parson's Daughter* (1833): "Miss Budd, although she said nothing, looked vinegar and *verjuice*." Used in, or as, medicine from the 14th century, it sometimes contained unripened olive oil and such acidic fruit juices as lemons, oranges, pomegranates and quinces, often

fermented. Other sources described the inclusion of "crab juice" or pork broth. Along with its topical application for venereal diseases, Nicholas Culpepper's *Complete Herbal* (1653) recommended it, saying: "For a canker in the mouth, wash the mouth often with verjuice."

dressing-gong

One rung as the signal for dressing for dinner.

—Sir James Murray's *New English Dictionary*, 1897

The Sound of the Dressing Gong

Lady Diana, a popular columnist, magazine editor, actress and socialite, who was active in the influential group of intellectuals and aristocrats known as "The Coterie."

The above-mentioned *dressing-gong* was once commonly employed in a custom found in large households. About an hour before dinner, the dressing-gong was sounded to inform house guests that it was time to return to their rooms and prepare for the luncheon or dinner meal. Later in life, Lady Diana recalled a gong-servant at Belvoir Castle in Leicestershire around 1900: "The gong-man was an old retainer, one of those numberless ranks of domestic servants which have completely disappeared and today seem fabulous [imagined]. He was admittedly very old; he wore a white beard to his waist. Three times a day he rang the gong — for luncheon, for dressing-time, for dinner. He would walk down the interminable passages, his livery hanging loosely on his bent old bones, clutching his gong with one hand and with the other feebly brandishing the padded knobbed stick with which he struck it. Every corridor had to be warned, and the towers too. So I suppose he banged on and off for ten minutes, thrice daily."

Drinking and Smoking

I drink to make other people more interesting.

—Ernest Hemingway (1899–1961)

aleconner

An officer appointed . . . to look to the assize and goodness of bread, ale, and beer.

—John Kersey's *New English Dictionary*, 1772

The aleconners are authorised to search for, destroy, seize, and take away all unwholesome provisions, false balances, short weights and measures . . . and examine the quality of beer, ale, &c. and the materials of which it is made.

—William Robinson's *History and Antiquities of Tottenham High Cross*, 1818

Quality Control for Beer

According to Peter Ditchfield's *Old English Customs* (1896), when two "ale-tasters" are selected in late October, "they are bound to visit all the public houses in Dalton [England] and taste the ale, their omission of any house being met with a fine. They make a report, and those having the best ale are awarded a red ribbon, the second best obtaining a blue ribbon. . . . It is said that this custom dates from the time when the Abbot of Furness was supplied with ale from Dalton, and this was regularly tasted by specially appointed ale-tasters."

A European test (shown here) used by aleconners was to pour a

bit of ale onto a pub's bench. Wearing a pair of leather breeches, the official would sit in the beer for thirty minutes and then arise. If his trousers stuck to the bench, the brewer would be fined for serving a brew with too much sugar.

knight of the vapour

A smoker.

—Albert Hyamson's *Dictionary of English Phrases*, 1922

Whiffler, a smoker of tobacco; hence, a person of no consequence.

—Ebenezer Brewer's *Dictionary of Phrase and Fable*, 1898

Health Benefits of Tobacco

In his health treatise, *A Brief and Accurate Treatise Concerning the Taking of the Fume of Tobacco, which Very Many in these Dayes Doe too too Licenciously Use* (1650), Thomas Venner sang the praises of tobacco, even for children, saying, "It helpeth the brain that is over cold and moist, reducing it by its heating and drying faculty. . . . It taketh away rheumes and windinesse of the head, and is profitable for all cold affects of the brain and sinews by resolving and consuming the crude and windy superfluities of those parts. It doth expell melancholy, and excite lumpish spirits; it helpeth pains of the teeth, swellings of the gummes, and aches of the joints. It expelleth winde and preventeth putrefaction of humors by drying up the crudities of the body . . . and for all cold and moist affects of the stomack, breast, and lungs. It is a speedy remedy . . . in an infant, remov[ing] windy torments of the stomack and bowels that proceed of crude humors, and helpeth crude fits of the mother. In a word it is, being rightly used, available against all cold and moist distemperatures."

tears of the tankard

The drippings of liquor on a man's waistcoat.

—Francis Grose's *Classical Dictionary of the Vulgar Tongue*, 1796

Thoughts of Martin Luther

(1483–1546), German religious reformer. He once commented on the forerunner of modern science: "Alchemy I like very well. I like it not only for the profits it brings in melting metals, in decocting, preparing, extracting, and distilling herbs and roots. I like it also for the sake of allegory and secret signification, which is exceedingly fine, touching the resurrection of the dead on the last day."

Edmund Fillingham King's *Ten Thousand Wonderful Things* (c. 1853) described Luther's ornately carved drinking tankard (shown here): "This interesting relic of the great reformer is of ivory, very richly carved and mounted in silver gilt. There are six medallions on its surface which consist, however, of a repetition of two subjects. The

 upper one represents the agony in the garden, and the Savior praying that the cup might pass from Him. The base represents the Lord's Supper, the centre dish being the incarnation of the bread. . . . This drinking vessel, independent of its artistic merit, was no doubt highly valued as a mere household possession. . . . On the lid, in old characters, is the following: *M. L. MDXXIIII.*"

all sorts

A slang term designating the drippings of glasses in saloons, collected and sold at half-price to drinkers who are not overly particular.

—Sylva Clapin's *New Dictionary of Americanisms*, 1902

A term used in taverns or beer-shops to denote a beverage composed of remnants of various liquors mixed together.

—William Whitney's *Century Dictionary*, 1889

The leavings of [tavern] glasses, poured together and sold cheap.

—Mitford Mathews's *Dictionary of Americanisms*, 1956

Alls, the refuse of *all sorts* of spirits drained from [patrons' unfinished] glasses, or spilt in drawing. The mixture is sold in gin-houses at a cheap rate.

—Ebenezer Brewer's *Dictionary of Phrase and Fable*, 1898

Recycling Beer

George Sala's *Gaslight and Daylight* (1859) described a piece of tavern hardware employed to collect the varied components of *all sorts*: "A counter perforated in elaborately-pricked patterns, like a convivial shroud, apparently for ornament but ready for the purpose of allowing the drainings, overflowings, and outspillings of the . . . glasses to drop through. . . . Being collected with sundry washings, and a dash, perhaps, of fresh material . . . the thrifty landlord dispensed [it] to his customers under the title of *all sorts*."

dog-nose

A cordial composed of warm porter, moist sugar, gin, and nutmeg.

—James Halliwell's *Dictionary of Archaic and Provincial Words*, 1855

England's Gin Plague

In 1736, the British Parliament passed the Gin Act. We read in Frederick Hackwood's *Inns, Ales and Drinking Customs of Old England* (1909): "The madness for gin-drinking attained such a height [that] the government became seriously alarmed and set about legislation for checking it. . . . In London, one house in every four was a gin-shop, for the spirit was retailed by tradesmen who dealt in other commodities. It was even sold from stables, sheds, and wheelbarrows.

"Gin was so cheap it was not uncommon for a sign to read, 'Here a man may get drunk for a penny, and dead drunk for two pence.' In 1736, a tax of twenty shillings a gallon was put on gin, and every retailer of it was compelled to pay £50 for a license. . . . On the day the Act came into force . . . hooting mobs assembled round the dens where they could no longer get drunk for a copper, and the last [article of clothing] was pawned to obtain a drink of the beloved liquor. Such was the popular resentment against the Gin Act that it was thought advisable for some days to mount a double guard at Kensington Palace. . . . For several years Gin Riots were constantly taking place."

broken beer

Remnants of beer. *Broken victuals* is still a common expression, but *broken beer* sounds strange, as hardly applicable to liquids. Yet it occurs.

—Robert Nares's *Glossary of the Works of English Authors,* 1859

Fine Points of Beer Quaffing

Thomas Venner's *Via Recta: A Treatise . . . for Attaining to a Long and Healthfull Life* (1650) weighed in on the health implications of the long-running debate over the serving-temperature of beer: "Some may demand whether it be better to drink their beer cold or a little warmed, especially in the winter season. Whereto I answer that I see no good reason to approve the drinking thereof warme, as I know some to do, not only in winter but almost all the yeare, for it is nauseous and fulsome to the stomack, and therefore it cannot but dull the appetite and rather hurt than further the concoction.

"Moreover it doth not so well quench the thirsy, temper the natural heat, refresheth, and cool the inward parts as if it is taken cold. But warme drink is to be allowed to cold, aged bodies, and so such as are of a melancholy phlegmatick temperature, and that have weak sinews and joynts, and that are troubled with the tooth-ach. And for such as are subject to the gowt and wind-colick, or are troubled with the hoarsenesse and diseases of the throat and lungs, it is very good to take their drink a little warmed. . . . But to all other[s] it is hurtfull."

potvaliant

Made daring by excessive drinking.
—Daniel Fenning's *Royal English Dictionary*, 1775

Temulency, drunkenness. *Temulentine*, drunken.
—Elisha Coles's *An English Dictionary*, 1713

European Spirits

According to Frederick Hackwood's *Inns, Ales and Drinking Customs of Old England* (1909), "By the end of the 15th century, brandy had become an important article of manufacture in the wine-producing countries of the Continent, and the habit of drinking spirits began to spread through Europe. It is asserted by the antiquary Camden [1551–1623] that the English troops employed in the Low Countries were mainly responsible for introducing the habit of drinking spirits into England. . . . The phrase 'Dutch courage,' as an equivalent for being *potvaliant* [see above], is a well-known slang term reflecting on the drinking habits of Dutch fighting men of old time. . . . In the 16th century, the use of distilled spirits spread over the continent of

Europe and thence was introduced into the American colonies. Under the name of 'brandy,' it had previously been introduced into Ireland with such disastrous effects that the government had been compelled to prohibit its manufacture. On the Continent it was prepared from grapes, and in Spain and Italy was sold as a cordial."

woofits

The unpleasant aftereffects of overindulgence, especially drinking.

—Lester Berrey's *American Thesaurus of Slang*, 1942

Barley-fever, illness caused by intemperence.

—Joseph Shipley's *Dictionary of Early English*, 1955

Mardi Gras Hangover Day

The New World celebration of Mardi Gras began in Plaquemines Parish, south of New Orleans in 1699. In *America Revisited* (1883), George Augustus Sala reported on day-after effects in that city: "There seemed to be some difficulty, on the Wednesday and Thursday succeeding Mardi Gras, in convincing the good people of New Orleans that Carnival was over, that Lent had begun, and that Fun was as dead as Queen Anne. On the French side of Canal Street, the Creoles, being orthodox Romanists [Catholics] meekly accepted the inevitable, furled their flags, laid by their masks, and made up their minds for forty days' abstinence from gaiety and conviviality — to be alleviated perchance by a trifling 'spurt' of music and dancing at the *Mi-carême* [a mid-Lent relaxation of rules practiced by the French]. Otherwise . . . the clerical gentlemen with tonsures and in cassocks, would have things all their own way until Easter. It is equally true that so early as the morrow of Mardi Gras, the process of depopulation was visible to a phenomenal extent at all the hotels."

quafftide

Time of drinking.

—T. Lewis Davies's *Supplementary English Glossary*, 1881

Prohibition Takes Root

In 1920, the Volstead Act went into effect in America, a year after the legislation banning the sale of alcoholic beverages, collectively still known as "Prohibition," was passed by the U.S. Congress. In the intervening year — intended to give breweries, wineries and distilleries time to transition to another business — beer, wine and spirits were of course hoarded, greatly increasing their sales and value. The Chicago-based drug chain Walgreen's positioned itself to take full advantage of this situation, creating a variety of alcohol-based pseudo-medicines which could still be sold legally after this date. In fact, according to historians, it actually became easier to buy a drink after the adoption of Prohibition laws because so many unlicensed taverns sprang up.

When Prohibition ended in 1933, many rules were added, such as  that alcohol-serving establishments could not be located near churches, schools, and hospitals. But on principle, one San Francisco judge refused to convict small-scale violators of Prohibition laws brought before him. He not only overturned the arrests but also returned the alcoholic evidence to its owners.

insufflation

The act of blowing a gas or vapour into a cavity of the body, as when tobacco smoke is injected into the rectum.

—Richard Hoblyn's *Medical Dictionary*, 1859

From Latin *sufflatus*, blown up, puffed out.

—Rev. James Stormonth's *Dictionary of the English Language*, 1884

Saving Lives with Tobacco?

In 1774, London's Royal Humane Society was founded as the Humane Society for the Recovery of Persons Apparently Drowned. According to the Society website's FAQ section, it was as also dubbed The Institution for Affording Immediate Relief to Persons Apparently Dead from Drowning. This organization's mission was initially to reduce drowning deaths, especially along the Thames, and to this end, until about 1810, they employed a "tobacco resuscitator kit," which directed tobacco smoke into the rectums of victims to stimulate and warm them. To make these devices readily available when needed, boxed kits were mounted along the Thames by the Society, much as unsinkable life rings are now set out. An elegant example of this curious apparatus — made of boxwood and brass, and fitted with a small leather bellow — has been on display in London's Wellcome Collection.

thumb-brewed

Approaching maturity. From Latin *maturesco*, to become ripe.

—Daniel Lyons's *American Dictionary of the English Language*, 1897

To regulate the fermentation, brewers determined the heat in brewing by dipping the thumb into the vat. Ale and beer brewed in this maker was called *thumb-brewed*.

—George Stimpson's *Book About A Thousand Things*, 1946

Brewing Beer the Old-Fashioned Way

Robley Dunglison's *Dictionary of Medical Science* (1844) offered this recipe for brewing "cock ale," a potent and "provocative" elixir: "Take ten gallons of ale and a large cock, the older the better; parboil the cock, flay him and stamp him in a stone mortar till his bones are broken then put the cock into two quarts of sack [sherry] and put to it three pounds of raisins of the sun, some blades of mace, and a few cloves. Put all these into a canvas bag and a little before you find the ale has done working; put the ale and bag together into a vessel; in a week or nine days time, bottle it up. Fill the bottle but just above the neck and give it the same time to ripen as other ale."

Alice Morse Earle's *Stagecoach and Tavern Days* (1900) showed that the wide array of specialty beers available in today's microbreweries has a long history. Here she writes of those from two centuries ago: "Some New England taverns were famous for their ... beer, boiled with scores of roots and herbs, with birch, spruce, or sassafras bark, with pumpkin and apple parings, with sweetening of molasses or maple syrup, or beet tops and other makeshifts."

flap-dragons

Small combustible bodies . . . floated in a glass of liquor, which an experienced toper swallowed unharmed, while still blazing.

—Isaac D'Israeli's *Curiosities of Literature*, 1866

This was a common amusement in former times, but now nearly obsolete. *Flap-dragon* was also a cant term for the *lues venerea*.

—James Halliwell's *Dictionary of Archaic and Provincial Words*, 1855

From *dragon*, supposed to breathe fire. [Mentioned in *Love's Labour's Lost*.]

—Samuel Johnson's *Dictionary of the English Language*, 1755

The Pub as Social Hub

Frederick Hackwood's *Inns, Ales and Drinking Customs of Old England* (1909) said, "The facilities offered by licensed houses for public meetings have long caused them to be used as educational and recreative institutions. Countless . . . musical societies have met, and still meet, at public-houses, not a few of which have become famous for their glee parties and philharmonic unions. Similarly, they have often been the birthplace of literary, scientific, and philosophical debating societies. Birmingham, for instance, as becomes the foremost city in Warwickshire, has some of its finest Shakespeare reading societies attached to licensed premises, as also many northern towns have Burns Societies similarly housed."

jiggs

Small dregs or sediment, as of a pot of coffee or a bottle of physic.

—Rev. Robert Forby's *Vocabulary of East Anglia*, 1830

Just Say No — to Coffee?

In 1909, Frederick Hackwood's *Inns, Ale, and Drinking Customs of Old England* described coffee's colorful history in Britain, remarking, "For a long time, coffee was regarded as a dangerous drug, and those who indulged too freely in the new beverage were looked upon almost as drunkards. It was ridiculed with such nicknames as *ninny-broth* and *turkey-gruel*.

"A petition was presented to Parliament in 1673 praying that coffee, tea, and brandy should be prohibited, as the use of these newer beverages interfered with the consumption of barley malt and wheat, native products of the country. The petitioners boldly asserted that the 'laborious people,' who constituted the majority of the population,

required to drink 'good strong beer and ale' which greatly refreshed their bodies after their hard labours, and that the flagon of strong beer, with which they refreshed themselves each morning and every evening, did them no great prejudice, hindered not their work, nor took away their senses. And while it cost them little money, it greatly promoted the consumption of homegrown grain, whereas the drinking of brandy destroyed many of His Majesty's subjects."

duffifie

To lay a bottle on its side for some time after its contents have been poured out, that it may be completely drained of the few drops remaining; Aberdeen. Elsewhere, one is said to "make the bottle confess."

—John Jamieson's *Etymological Dictionary of the Scottish Language*, 1808

Twenty Old Ways To Say 'Shnockered'

In 1736, American statesman and inventor Benjamin Franklin printed in the *Pennsylvania Gazette* 200 largely forgotten vernacular euphemisms for "drunk." These included: *pidgeon-ey'd, moon-ey'd, drunk as a wheelbarrow, half-way to Concord, crump-footed, double-tongu'd, dizzy as a goose, jambled, going to Jerusalem, contending with Pharaoh,* and *loose in the hilts* — originally a British expression involving mistaken anatomy. Beyond these, he or she: *smelt of an onion, froze his mouth, had a thump over the head with Sampson's jawbone, had been too free with Sir John Strawberry, drank till he gave up his half-penny, had got on his little hat, had been to Jericho* (or *Barbadoes*), and *had taken off his considering-cap.*

Franklin vouched for the authenticity of these localisms, writing, "The phrases in this dictionary are not borrow'd from foreign languages; neither are they collected from the writings of the learned, but gather'd wholly from the modern tavern conversation of tipplers."

crapulence

Drunkenness, sickness by intemperance.

—Samuel Johnson's *Dictionary of the English Language*, 1755

Crapulosity, inclination to drunkenness; or to gluttony. *Crapulous*, suffering from the effects of intemperance in drinking. *Crapulousness*, [the] quality of being crapulous. *Crapulenta*, pertaining to crapulence. [From] Latin *crapula*, excessive drinking, inebriation, intoxication.

—Sir James Murray's *New English Dictionary*, 1893

Americans Outquaffed Europeans?

In 1837, English naval captain Frederick Marryat penned these liquor-related observations along with some explanations, which were compiled and published two years later as *A Diary in America*: "I always did consider that the English and the Swiss were the two nations who most indulged in potations. But on my arrival in the United States I found that our descendants, in this point, most assuredly surpassed us altogether. Impartiality compels me to acknowledge the truth — we must, in this instance, submit to a national defeat. There are many causes for this. First, the heat of the climate; next, the coldness of the climate; add to these the cheapness of liquor in general, the early disenfranchisement of the youth from all parental control; and lastly, the pleasantness, amenity, and variety of the potations."

coffee-tea

Infusion of the leaves of the coffee-plant.

—Sir James Murray's *New English Dictionary*, 1893

Tea Time Comes of Age

Henry Graham's *The Social Life of Scotland in the Eighteenth Century* (1899) (1899) explained why tea — like some drugs today — was considered both unpatriotic and a road to degradation: "The introduction of tea was met with animosity by haters of newfangled beverages and the patriotic lovers of native products. Town councils, heritors [heirs], and ministers equally denounced it, and parishes afflicted with smuggling entered into resolutions to abstain from tea just as people take pledges today against alcoholic beverages. In 1744 the heritors of East Lothian complained that 'the luxurious and expensive way of living has shamefully crept in upon all classes of people.' ... The drinking of tea, especially among people of the lower rank, has arrived at an extravagant excess to the hurt of families by loss of their time, increase of their expense, and neglect of a diet more suitable to their health and station."

In *Salad for the Solitary and the Social* (1853) Frederick Saunders wrote: "Tea was [first] used medicinally, and it was not until the end of the 17th century that it was indulged in as a beverage. The first brewers of tea were often perplexed with the preparation. ... After boiling the tea they sat down to eat the leaves with butter and salt."

Glimpses of Britain

There is nothing so bad or so good that you will not find Englishmen doing it — but you will never find an Englishman in the wrong. He does everything on principle. He fights you on patriotic principles; he robs you on business principles; and he enslaves you on imperial principles.

—George Bernard Shaw's play, *The Man of Destiny*, 1897

skare on

To splice two pieces of wood together. From Jutland
Danish *at skarre ved*, to join two pieces together.
—Rev. Marmaduke Morris's *Yorkshire Folk-Talk*, 1892

Would It Have Been *Frangland* or *Englance*?

In 1956, French Prime Minister Guy Mollet proposed a bizarre-
sounding French-British merger to his English counterpart,
Sir Antony Eden. The "Declaration of Union" suggested that
longtime rivals Britain and France become a single nation with
joint citizenship, government, currency, and armed forces, and no
customs procedures. But apparently it was the British, under Winston
Churchill, who were the first to broach the subject in 1940 after
France's capitulation to the Nazis, according to secret documents.
This shocking idea, which even Gen. Charles de Gaulle reluctantly
embraced as an "indissoluble union," was declassified in the late
1980s, but it only gathered dust in Britain's National Archives until
January 2007.

One of the ironies of this misguided
diplomacy was that Mollet was a socialist
who considered the execution of French
King Louis XVI and his opulence-
addicted family and thousands of
supporters a highlight in French
history. But one document said he "had
not thought there need be difficulty over
France accepting the headship of her
Majesty [Elizabeth II]."

starry-gazy-pie

A pie [still] made of [herring-like] pilchards and leeks, the heads of the pilchards appearing throughout the crust as if they were studying the sky.

—James Halliwell's *Dictionary of Archaic and Provincial Words*, 1855

Saluting the Humble Leek

Cleverly, St. David had his sixth-century warriors fasten leeks to their hats to enable them to distinguish and defeat the Saxons in hand-to-hand combat. Today, leeks are found on the Welsh flag as well as some £1 British coins to remind us of this, although the daffodil remains the official symbol of Wales.

Heroics aside, William Turner's *Herbal* (1568) cautioned would-be consumers of the leek's dark side: "The leek breedeth wind and evil juice, and maketh heavy dreams; it stirreth a man to make water and is good for the belly. But if you would boil a leek in two waters, and afterwards steep it in cold water, it will be less windy than before." More recently, "to eat the leek" indicated the embarrassed retraction of a statement, much like "eating crow." It was used in this regard in a passage from Shakespeare's *Henry V*: "Hee is come to me, and prings me pread and sault yesterday; looke you, and bid me *eate my leeke*."

fromward

Away from; the contrary of toward; [derived from] Saxon *fram* [from] and *weard* [towards].

—John Boag's *Imperial Lexicon of the English Language*, c. 1850

Departing, about to depart; only Old English [c. 888–1000]. Of time, onward from a given date.

—Sir James Murray's *New English Dictionary*, 1897

England's Mail Service Begun

The first mail-coach left London at eight o'clock in the morning on 8th August, 1764 and arrived at Bristol at eleven at night. Till then, the post office had sent mails by passenger coaches which, with the view of picking up fares, ran at any time which suited the owner or the driver, the guard or the ostler, the squire or my lady. It was John Palmer, of Bath, who conceived the idea of running coaches with the special object of carrying the mails. He went to Mr. Pitt and succeeded in convincing him that the scheme would not only be of great advantage to letter-writers but also remunerative to the government, and from that time forward mail-coaches continued to run until they were superseded by railway trains.

—Basil Hargrave's *Origins and Meanings of Popular Phrases and Names*, 1925

lubberland

A slang term anciently applied to London — substituted for *Cocaigne* by the poets and wits of the 16th century. *Lud's Town*, a name sometimes anciently given to London [was] so called after *Lud*, a mythical king of England. "And on the gates of Lud's Town set your heads." Shakespeare's *Cymbeline*.

—Henry Frederic Reddall's *Fact, Fancy, and Fable*, 1889

Another View of London

After a stroll about London in 1857, during a four-year stint as American consul in England, curmudgeonly Massachusetts author Nathaniel Hawthorne penned this mixed impression in his journal: "Very dull and dreary the city looked, and not in the least gay and lively, even where the throng was thickest and most brisk. As I trudged along, my reflection was that never was there a dingier, uglier, less picturesque city than London, and that it is really wonderful [surprising] that so much brick and stone have been built up with so poor a result. Yet these old names of the city — Fleet-street, Ludgate Hill, the Strand — used to throw a glory over these homely precincts when I first saw them."

But on that same day Hawthorne was cheered by the countryside, adding to his entry, "Everywhere the immortal verdure [greenery] of England [was] scarcely less perfect than in June, so far as the fields are concerned, though the foliage of the trees presents much the same hues as those of our [New England] forests."

ruricolist

An inhabitant of the country.

—Daniel Fenning's *The Royal English Dictionary*, 1775

The English Countryside

Beginning with his 1815 visit, New York-trained lawyer, local historian and writer Washington Irving (1783–1859) adored England, and traveled there to gather material for a glowing essay on country life, in which he wrote: "What most delights me is the creative talent with which the English decorate the unostentatious abodes of middle life. The rudest habitation, the most unpromising and scanty portion of land, in the hands of an Englishman of taste, becomes a little paradise. With a nicely discriminating eye, he seizes at once upon its capabilities, and pictures in his mind the future landscape. The sterile spot grows into loveliness under his hand, and yet the operations of art which produce the effect are scarcely to be perceived. The cherishing and training of some trees, the cautious pruning of others, the nice distribution of flowers and plants of tender and graceful foliage, the introduction of a green slope of velvet turf, the partial opening to a peep of blue distance, or silver gleam of water — all these are managed with a delicate tact, a pervading yet quiet assiduity, like the magic touchings with which a painter finishes up a favorite picture."

centesimation

A military punishment for desertion, mutiny, or the like, where one person in a hundred is selected for execution.
—Rev. John Boag's *Imperial Lexicon of the English Language*, c. 1850

Scottish Culture Shock

In 1688, England's James II fled to France. His supporters rebelled at James's exile and staged intermittent uprisings that lasted until 1746. As a result, the Scots were punished for these so-called "Jacobite invasions" in a number of ways. They were prohibited from legally possessing weapons, playing their bagpipes, and speaking the Gaelic language openly.

Beyond these restrictions, men were not permitted to wear such garments as kilts, and women were denied their tartan arisaid dresses. In this regard, Tobias Smollett's novel, *The Expedition of Humphry Clinker* (1771), told how men were "deprived of their ancient garb, which was both graceful and convenient; and what is a greater hardship still, they are compelled to wear breeches, a restraint which they cannot bear with any degree of patience. . . . They are even debarred the use of their striped stuff called Tartane, which was their own manufacture, prized by them above all velvets, brocades, and tissues of Europe and Asia." This engraving is by Albrecht Dürer, 1514.

autonomasy

In rhetoric, a word of common or general signification used for the name of a particular thing, as . . . "the City," instead of London.

—John Boag's *Imperial Lexicon of the English Language*, c. 1850

Londonoy, a Londoner; Chaucer.

—James Halliwell's *Dictionary of Archaic and Provincial Words*, 1855

Inexhaustible London

In 1763, James Boswell discussed London with his mentor and friend, Samuel Johnson, later including some of Dr. Johnson's comments in his biography: "Sir, if you wish to have a notion of the magnitude of this city, you must not be satisfied with seeing its great streets and squares, but must survey the innumerable little lanes and courts. It is not in the showy evolutions of buildings, but in the multiplicity of human habitations which are crowded together, that the wonderful immensity of London consists. I have often amused myself with thinking how different a place London is to different people. They, whose narrow

 minds are contracted to the consideration of some one pursuit, view it only through that medium. . . . But the intellectual man is struck with it as comprehending the whole of human life in all its variety, the contemplation of which is inexhaustible." Johnson also warned, "Prepare for death, if here at night you roam, and sign your will before you sup from home."

immur

To enclose within walls; to surround with walls; to imprison; [from] Norman *emmurrer*.

—Rev. John Boag's *Imperial Lexicon of the English Language*, c. 1850

Charles Stewart Parnell

As he was a well-to-do landlord and a Member of Parliament, Parnell became known as the "uncrowned king of Ireland." He was arrested and kept in Dublin's notoriously deplorable Kilmainham Gaol, but because he was a wealthy landowner, he was housed in an oversized cell and was allowed to have visitors, who brought him good food and drink. He was also permitted to have regular exercise and was even granted leave to undertake excursions to London and Paris. Despite these privileges, Parnell was relentless in achieving independence for Ireland, and is buried in Dublin's Glasnevin Cemetery alongside such other revolutionary heroes as Michael Collins, Daniel O'Connell, and Éamon de Valera.

Testifying before the Royal Commission on Prisons in Ireland in 1884, Parnell reported, "One thing that struck me in Kilmainham was the semi-starved aspect which all the convicted prisoners presented. They seemed to be utterly dejected and weak, and unable to undergo any amount of physical fatigue. . . . I do not think that we are entitled to enfeeble the bodies of prisoners in order to reform their minds, or with a view of maintaining discipline amongst them."

riverfinders

When the tide is sufficiently low they scatter themselves along the shore, separating from each other, and soon disappear among the craft lying about in every direction. This is the case on both sides of the river [Thames] . . . extending as far as Vauxhall Bridge and Woolwich.

—Henry Mayhew's *London Labour and the London Poor*, 1861

Mudlark, a man or woman who, with clothes tucked above the knee, grovels through the mud on the banks of the Thames when the tide is low, for silver or pewter spoons, old bottles, pieces of iron, coal, or any articles of the least value deposited by the retiring tide, either from passing ships or the sewers.

—John Camden *Hotten's Slang Dictionary*, 1887

London's First Underground

During the 1840s and 1850s, Henry Mayhew English social chronicler and the founder of *Punch* traveled throughout Dickens's London, mostly on foot, gathering and sifting through his firsthand interviews with members of the working class and underworld to create his respected London labor study. He commented about one of his favorite groups of salvagers: "The sewer-hunters, strange as it may

 appear, are certainly smart fellows, and take decided precedence of all the other 'finders' of London . . . on account of the skill and courage they manifest in the pursuit of their dangerous employment."

welk

To decline; to fade; to decay; to fall; to contract; to shorten; [from] German *welken*, to wither.

—Rev. John Boag's *Imperial Lexicon of the English Language*, c. 1850

Slamper-up, to collapse. *Slampy*, soft and wet. [From] *slamp*, limp, weakly, tottering.

—Francis Taylor's *The Folk-Speak of South Lancashire*, 1901

The Demise of Dunwich

In 1919, the last tower of All Saints' Church in rural Dunwich, England, collapsed into the North Sea. Its medieval remains, southeast of Norwich, were mostly destroyed by 1750 but not discovered until 1971. At that time historian Stuart Bacon came across its ruins during a diving expedition, encouraging him to also locate remnants of St. Peter's Church two years later in thirty feet of water. In examining this undersea museum and reviewing Roman and Church records, archeologists found that Dunwich had been East Anglia's capital during the Roman occupation of Britain fifteen centuries earlier. By that time, storms had begun to reclaim the town's stone buildings one by one, eventually consuming eight churches and hundreds of smaller buildings. Although the population of this so-called "rotten borough" declined steadily to about 237 by the mid-1800s, a curious and outdated method of determining members of Parliament allowed it to retain two represent- atives until the 1832 Reform Act.

clashmaclavers

Low, idle, scandalous tales.

—John Mactaggart's *Scottish Gallovidian Encyclopedia*, 1824

The Canterbury Pilgrims Depart

In April 1387, 29 fictional travelers invented by Geoffrey Chaucer gathered in Southwark's Tabard Inn, across the Thames from London, for their celebrated 60-mile pilgrimage to the shrine of St. Thomas Becket in Kent. Many contributed stories along the way — the famous "Canterbury tales." Six centuries later, Chaucer's Middle English is still easily readable, as in this passage from the prologue describing the group:

> *Redy to wenden on my pilgrimage*
> *To Caunterbury with ful devout corage,*
> *At night was come in-to that hostelrye*
> *Wel nyne and twenty in a companye.*

Although these accounts would come to be regarded as literary treasures by the 16th century, the term "Canterbury tale" became synonymous with a tedious or unbelievable story. According to James Greenough's *Words and Their Ways in English Speech* (1902), the equestrian term "cantering" came about as a shortened form of "Canterbury gallop" — an easy horse's pace. William Caxton's engraving (shown at left) of the dining pilgrims was included in his 1484 edition of the *Tales*.

aeroflation

Passing through the air in balloons.

—Noah Webster's *Compendious Dictionary of the English Language*, 1806

The Battle of Britain Begins

In 1940, the German Luftwaffe began an intensive but ultimately unsuccessful bombing assault on southern England to pave the way for an invasion that would never arrive. A century earlier, and many decades before the first heavier-than-air flying-machines, Alfred Lord Tennyson (shown here) envisioned aerial combat in his poem *Locksley Hall* (1842):

> For I dipt into the future, far as the human eye could see,
> Saw the vision of the world, and all the wonder that would be;
> Saw the heavens fill with commerce, argosies of magic sails,
> Pilots of the purple twilight, dropping down with costly bales;
> Heard the heavens fill with shouting, and there rain'd a ghastly dew
> From the nations' airy navies grappling in the central blue.

Imaginative Benjamin Franklin also foresaw an airborne military assault. He wrote in 1784, "Five thousand balloons, capable of raising two men each, could not cost more than five ships [yielding] 10,000 men descending from the clouds before a force could be brought together to repel them."

gardyloo!

A common cry in former days of the dwellers in the high flats of Edinburgh, who were in the habit of throwing urine, slops, &c. out of the window. From French *garde l'eau*, beware of the water.

—T. Ellwood Zell's *Encyclopedia of Knowledge and Language*, 1871

Sensational Edinburgh

In his *Journal of a Tour to the Hebrides* (1785), a travel memoir of a trip he took with his friend Samuel Johnson, James Boswell recalled this stenchy adventure in Scotland's capital in 1773: "Mr. Johnson and I walked arm-in-arm up the High Street. . . . I could not prevent his being assailed by the evening effluvia of Edinburgh. I heard a late baronet of some distinction observe that walking the streets of Edinburgh at night was pretty perilous and a good deal odiferous."

Boswell continued, "The peril is much abated by the care which the magistrates have taken to enforce the city laws against throwing foul water from the windows; but from the structure of the houses

 in the old town, which consists of many storeys in each of which a different family lives, and there being no covered sewers, the odour still continues. A zealous Scotsman would have wished Mr. Johnson to be without one of his five senses upon this occasion. As we marched slowly along, he grumbled in my ear, 'I smell you in the dark'."

hallibrash

A great blaze. Northern England.

—Francis Grose's *Provincial Glossary*, 1811

The Great Fire of London

began on September 2, 1666 and destroyed 85% of London's buildings. But in terms of casualties, it was not London's worst, that distinction falling to a conflagration in 1212, which claimed about 12,000 lives. The more recent fire began without much notice, prompting the Lord Mayor to dismiss it at first as one so small that, in his words, "a woman might piss it out." Until this disaster, individual parishes were responsible for fire protection, but from 1666 until 1833, London insurance companies hired private fire brigades for their clients' buildings. So the firefighting companies would sometimes douse a fire at a building with metal insurance-status badges displayed, while leaving a neighbor's uninsured structure ablaze, before the advent of house numbering in the 1840s.

Diarist John Evelyn penned this description of the 1666 fire: "All the sky was of a fiery aspect, like the top of a burning oven, and the light seen above forty miles roundabout for many nights. God grant mine eyes may never behold the like, who now saw above 10,000 houses in one flame!" On rebuilding the city, interest was expressed in creating grand boulevards, as in Paris now, but planners chose to retain much of London's medieval street plan.

sabberday

A corruption of "Sabbath day," erroneously used for Sunday.

—Richard Thornton's *American Glossary*, 1912

Sabbaday-houses, formerly ... houses near a church or meeting-houses, used as places of recess by worshippers coming from long distances.

—Sylva Clapin's *New Dictionary of Americanisms*, 1902

Sundays in the Country

Joseph Addison thought about the Sabbath in July 1711, later publishing his reflections in *The Spectator:* "I am always very well pleased with a country Sunday, and think, if keeping holy the Seventh Day were only a human institution, it would have been the best method that could have been thought of for polishing and civilising mankind. It is certain the country people would soon degenerate into ... savages and barbarians were there not such frequent returns of a stated time in which the whole village meet[s] together with their best faces and in their cleanliest habits, to converse with one another and join together in adoration of the Supreme Being. Sunday clears away the rust of the whole week, not only as it refreshes in their minds the notions of religion, but as it puts both the sexes upon appearing

 in their most agreeable forms and exerting all such qualities as are apt to give them a figure in the eye of the village. A country fellow distinguishes himself as much in the churchyard as a citizen does upon the [ex]change, the whole parish politics being generally discussed in that place."

elucubrate

To produce a literary work by expenditure of "midnight oil." Formed of Latin *elucubrare*, to compose by lamplight.

—Sir James Murray's *New English Dictionary*, 1901

To do a thing by candlelight.

—Henry Cockeram's *Interpreter of Hard English Words*, 1623

The Beginning of London's Gaslight Era

After bearing the embarrassment of being Europe's worst-lit capital for decades, London's Pall Mall became the first English street to glow with gaslight in 1807. Robert Chambers's *Book of Days* (1864) discussed this development two centuries ago, including a curious misconception about gas: "When we consider that gaslight has since been extended all over London, over nearly every town of above a thousand inhabitants in the empire, and pretty generally throughout the towns of both Europe and America, . . .

it becomes curious to observe the great hesitation expressed in the scientific and popular literature of 1807–09 regarding the possibility of applying it economically to general use. . . . Gas-lighting had a ridiculous objection to contend with. It was generally assumed that the pipes conveying gas would be hot, and people used to touch them cautiously, under the belief that a careless touch would burn them."

Writing, Painting and Music

Writing is a form of therapy. Sometimes I wonder how all those who do not write, compose or paint can manage to escape the madness, melancholia, the panic and fear which is inherent in a human situation.

—English novelist Graham Green's
Ways of Escape, 1980

The sounds of a fiddle.

—Thomas Wright's *Dictionary of Obsolete and Provincial English*, 1857

Bull-fiddle, Americanese for a violincello [also *baritone fiddle*; now *cello*].

— George Sala's *America Revisited*, 1883

Handel's *Water Music* Premieres — Three Times

In 1717 — 7/17/1717 to be exact — George Frideric Handel introduced his *Water Musick*, conducting about fifty players on one royal pleasure barge, while the king listened from another, as they plied the Thames upriver from near Whitehall and back. One of Handel's challenges was to maintain a reasonable volume, since the distance between the boats varied. Although the composition was essentially a suite of dances, no dancing is known to have taken place during the elaborate river party. Another reason for this festivity was the hope of German-born King George I (caricatured here trying on his crown) that appearing in public might help ingratiate him to his subjects. A Prussian legate who attended the event wrote: "Next to the king's barge was that of the musicians who played on all kinds of instruments, trumpets, horns, hautboys, bassoons, German flutes, French flutes, violins, and basses. . . . His Majesty approved of it so greatly that he caused it to be repeated [twice]. . . . The number of barges and of boats filled with people desirous of hearing was beyond counting."

dunduckytimur

A dull, indescribable colour. *Dundy*, of a dull colour, as *dundy* grey. From Anglo-Saxon *dun*.

—John Greaves Nall's *Glossary of the Dialect of East Anglia*, 1866

Lasting Impressions

The works of French painter Claude Monet (1840–1926) were considered amateurish, unfinished and even grotesque by most orthodox critics and buyers alike until at least the 1880s. One pundit in particular wrote of a Monet painting, "It verges on sheer lunacy." Another scoffed at the Impressionists as a group, saying, "One must pity these misguided people."

But Monet was serious about capturing the effects of light on his various subjects regardless of circumstances. He once convinced attendants at Paris's Gare St. Lazare to allow him to set up his easel among the baggage and trackside hustle-bustle to paint the steam coming from trains. On another occasion he found himself needing to rent a row of two dozen poplar trees along France's Epte River to delay woodcutters who had arrived to cut them before he had finished a series of paintings. During a wintertime painting expedition, he was approached by a group of walkers, one of whom recalled, "It was cold enough to split rocks. We glimpsed a little heater, then an easel, then a gentleman swathed in three overcoats, gloved hands, his face half frozen. It was Monsieur Monet studying an aspect of the snow."

bowdlerize

To emasculate through squeamishness [introduced in 1836; still heard occasionally].

—John Camden Hotten's *Slang Dictionary*, 1887

The Influence of Thomas Bowdler

(1754–1825) was first noticed in a censored version of Shakespeare's works he published in 1807, and with it Bowdler launched the first attempts at literary censorship. This publication unexpectedly set off an avalanche of 19th-century cleansings. The original bowdlerizer was Scottish poet Allan Ramsay, who in 1724 "cleaned up" a collection of his own poems without being prodded. By 1850, seven chastened editions of the Bard's plays had been done, and by 1900, nearly 50 altered editions had been produced, with another planned by Lewis Carroll before Carroll's death.

Victorian do-gooders believed that condensing these writings represented moral progress over their coarser predecessors, including Shakespeare's works. Most of the Nurse's lines were snipped out in *Romeo and Juliet*, for example. In a like manner, other classics underwent tidying excisions, including *Robinson Crusoe* in 1826 and *Tom Jones* in 1896. Jane Austen sidestepped censorship by rewording a single reference to "bastards" in the 1813 edition of her *Sense and Sensibility*. Mild Walt Whitman (shown here), who was often castigated for his frank sexual references, wrote, "Damn expurgated books! The dirtiest book of all is the expurgated book."

drumsler

A drummer. A form corrupted from . . . Dutch *trommelslager*.

—Walter Skeat's *Glossary of Tudor and Stuart Words*, 1914

Haydn Becomes a Father

Franz Joseph Haydn (1732–1809) became known as the "Father of the Symphony" for his 104 symphonies, despite his lack of formal musical training. His popular 100th symphony, which premiered in 1794, earned its martial moniker, the "Military Symphony," for its inclusion of several percussive Turkish Janissary band instruments — the bass drum, cymbals and triangle. These became standard orchestral instruments and were later adapted for jazz and rock ensembles.

But after the 100th's debut, one unimpressed reviewer wrote that the second movement evoked the "hellish roar of war increas[ing] to a climax of horrid sublimity." At that time, Turkish Janissary music had been in vogue for more than a decade. Mozart, for example, evoked these sounds in the overture and the "March of the Janissaries" in his opera, *The Abduction from the Seraglio* (1782), and in his celebrated "Rondo alla Turca," perhaps written as early as 1778. The Janissary style persisted in Western music for nearly 50 years in several of Beethoven's works, including the "Turkish March," in his *Ruins of Athens* (1812), and more subtly at the end of his 1824 masterwork *Ninth Symphony*. The Janissary band only began to decline in the mid-1800s, along with the Ottoman Empire.

melomania

A mania for music; hence, *melomaniac*, one who has a craze for music.

—Sir James Murray's *New English Dictionary*, 1908

Jazz Condemned in New Orleans

Popularized in the honky-tonks and brothels of old New Orleans, jazz has become America's most distinctive homegrown musical form. But before and after it took root, it was roundly condemned by various critics, such as Rev. Richard Yarrow of the Illinois Vigilance Association, who sounded this false alarm in 1923: "I can say from my own knowledge that about fifty percent of our young boys and girls from the age sixteen to twenty-five that land in the insane asylum these days are jazz-crazy dope fiends and public dance hall patrons. Jazz combinations — dope fiends and public dance halls — are the same. Where you find one, you will find the other."

Jazz rhythms were described as "sound, loud and meaningless," even by the *New Orleans Times-Picayune* in 1918, which warned that such sounds could have "an intoxicating effect, like crude colors and strong perfumes, the sight of flesh, or the [sadistic] pleasure in blood." Band leader John Philip Sousa (1854–1932), who gave us *The Stars and Stripes Forever* and other martial patriotic ditties, weighed in, saying, "Jazz is prostituted music, and the sooner we get rid of the stuff, the better for our boys and girls."

callipygian

Of, pertaining to, or having well-shaped or finely developed buttocks. The name of a famous statue of Venus. From Greek *kallos*, beauty, and *pyg*, buttocks. Hence, *callipygous*, *callipygously*.

—Sir James Murray's *New English Dictionary*, 1893

Young ladies stretching, writhing, *callipygously* stooping, to tie their sandals.

—Aldous Huxley's *After Many a Summer Dies the Swan*, 1939

Callipygæ, women largely composed behinde.

—Sir Thomas Browne's *Pseudodoxia Epidemica*, 1646

The Naked Truth

American author Nathaniel Hawthorne spent four years compiling observations of England in what would be published as his *English Notebooks*. In them he commented on the works of Yorkshire painter William Etty (1787–1849), whose nudes were often deemed indecent by critics: "The most disagreeable of English painters is Etty, who had a diseased appetite for women's flesh, and spent his whole life, apparently, in painting them with enormously developed bosoms and buttocks. I do not mind nudity in a modest and natural way, but Etty's women really thrust their nakedness upon you so with malice aforethought, and especially so enhance their posteriors that one feels inclined to kick them."

composuist

A writer, composer. This extraordinary word has been much used at some of our colleges, but seldom elsewhere. It is used in England among musicians.

—John Pickering's *Words and Phrases Peculiar to the United States*, 1816

The Rite of Spring

In 1913, avante-garde Russian composer Igor Stravinsky's once shockingly controversial ballet, *Le Sacre du Printemps*, opened in Paris, with Vaslav Nijinsky dancing the lead. The sensuality and dissonance of the score evoked whistles, howls, and catcalls, and eventually caused interruptions due to fistfights and pandemonium in the audience. Gendarmes were needed to restore order during the intermission, but only after Stravinsky had exited in disgust.

One music critic nicknamed it "Le Massacre du Printemps," while another, Carl Van Vechten, described the evening's events, including the unrestrained reaction of a gentleman sitting directly behind him: "The intense excitement under which he was laboring, thanks to the potent force of the music, betrayed itself presently when he began to beat rhythmically on the top of my head with his fists. My emotion was so great that I did not feel the blows for some time. They were perfectly synchronized with the beat of the music. When I did, I turned around. His apology was sincere. We had both been carried beyond ourselves."

nose-riders

Spectacles.

—Sir James Murray's *New English Dictionary*, 1908

Spurticles, spectacles.

—R. Pearse Chope's *The Dialect of Hartland, Devonshire*, 1891

Anachronisms of Shakespeare

In his *Cyclopedia of Anecdotes* (1883), Kazlitt Arvine pointed out these anachronisms from Shakespeare's plays: "Without noticing the blunders of some of his contemporaries, it may suffice to refer to a few of the glaring errors which may surprise some. In *The Comedy of Errors*, speaking of the ancient city of Ephesus, we find allusions made to ducats, marks, and guilders, as well as to an abbess of a nunnery, and also to a striking clock. In *King John* and *Macbeth*, we find reference made to cannon. In *Coriolanus*, reference is made to Alexander Cato and Galen, both of whom lived long subsequent to his day. Cassius, in *Julius Caesar*, speaks of a clock striking."

Arvine continued, "In *King Lear* [set in a mythical time before 1500] mistakes are as thick as leaves in Vallambrosa. Among others, Kent talks like a good Protestant of eating no fish, and Gloucester of not being compelled to the use of spectacles!" Voltaire was also unimpressed, and wrote, "English plays are like English puddings — nobody has any taste for them but the English."

claque

Applause by clapping the hands; persons paid for doing so. M. Sauton, in 1820, established in Paris an office to ensure the success of dramatic pieces. He was the first to organize the Parisian *claque*. The manager sends an order to his office for any number of *claquers* — sometimes for 500, or even more. The class is divided into *commissars*, those who commit the pieces to memory and are noisy in pointing out its merits; *rieurs*, who laugh at the puns and jokes; *pleureurs*, chiefly women, who are to hold their pocket-handkerchiefs to their eyes at the moving parts; *chatouilleurs*, who are to keep the audience in good humour; and *bisseurs*, who are to cry *bis!* [for] encores. The Romans had their Laudicœni.

—Ebenezer Brewer's *Dictionary of Phrase and Fable,* 1898

And the Crowd Went Wild

French poet and renowned Greek and Latin scholar, Jean Daurat (1508-1588) established a society for reforming the French language. During the 1820s, he also promoted Paris's claque (see above) system, which spread to La Scala in Milan, London's Covent Garden, New York's Metropolitan Opera House, and elsewhere. At first, claquers were merely given free tickets in exchange for their obsequious applause. But over time they became specialized, as mentioned above, and were overseen by a "chef de claque," who would also contact singers, maestros, and theater managers to demand extortion for restraining his people from booing performances.

punctualist

One that is very exact in observing forms and ceremonies. [From] *punctual*, consisting in a point.

—Noah Webster's *American Dictionary of the English Language*, 1828

Mark Twain as Critic

James Fenimore Cooper's famous novel, *The Deerslayer*, was ridiculed by Mark Twain in 1895, primarily for Cooper's imprecise choices of words. Twain specified more than 30 such terms, from the substitution of "verbal" for "oral" to the use of "mortified" instead of "disappointed." Twain compared writing with music making: "Cooper's word-sense was singularly dull. When a person has a poor ear for music he will flat and sharp right along without knowing it. He keeps *near* the tune, but [has] not the tune. When a person has a poor ear for words, the result is a literary flatting and sharping; you perceive what he is intending to say, but you also perceive that he does not say it. [Cooper's] ear was satisfied with the approximate words."

Elsewhere Twain sniped: "A work of art? It has no invention; it has no order, system, sequence, or result; it has no lifelikeness, no thrill, no stir, no seeming of reality; its characters are confusedly drawn, and by their acts and words they prove that they are not the sort of people the author claims; its humor is pathetic; its pathos is funny; its conversations are, oh, indescribable; its love-scenes odious." He summed it up, saying, "Its English is a crime against the language."

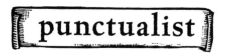

quisby

To say that a man is without money, or in poverty, some persons remark that he is . . . *quisby*, done up.

—Charles Dickens's *Household Words*, 1853

Doing quisby, not working; queer; not right; bankrupt.

—Sir James Murray's *New English Dictionary*, 1914

Artistic Perspiration

English littérateur George Lewes (1817–1878) who made a compelling argument that successful artists "depended more on perspiration than inspiration" several decades before hard-working Thomas Edison was reported to have said — more famously about 1902 — that "genius is one percent inspiration and ninety-nine percent perspiration." Lewes (shown here) stated it this way: "There is in the present day an overplus of raving about genius and its prescriptive rights of irresponsibility and its insubordination to all the laws of common sense. Common sense is so prosaic! Yet it appears from the history of art that the real men of genius did not rave about anything of the kind. They were resolute workers, not idle dreamers. They knew that their genius was not a frenzy, not a supernatural thing at all, but simply the colossal proportions of faculties which, in a lesser degree, the meanest of mankind shared with them. They knew that whatever it was, it would not enable them to accomplish with success the things they undertook unless they devoted their whole energies to the task."

stirps

Race; lineage; family; the origin or the founder of a family or race, early anglicized as *stirp, stirpe*. From Latin.
—C. A. M. Fennell's *Stanford Dictionary of Anglicised Words and Phrases*, 1964

To *count kin* with one, to compare one's pedigree with that of another. It is common for one who has perhaps been spoken of disrespectfully.
—John Jamieson's *Etymological Dictionary of the Scottish Language*, 1808

Ancientry, the honour of ancient lineage; the dignity of birth.
—Samuel Johnson's *Dictionary of the English Language*, 1755

Know Your Ancestors

Once while browsing in a shop of antiquities, four-time English prime minister William Gladstone (1809–1898) took a liking to a 17th-century portrait of a gentleman dressed in splendid Spanish attire. But after haggling with the shopkeeper, Gladstone concluded that the price was too high, and he decided against trying to purchase the picture. Some time later, he came across this same painting in the home of an ostentatious acquaintance, who told him that the subject was an ancestor who had served in Queen Elizabeth I's court. Responding to this disingenuous display of pretentious malarkey, Gladstone muttered mockingly to himself, "A few pounds less and he would've been my ancestor."

leden

The word not only meant the Latin language, but language in general — even that attributed to birds and beasts. Chaucer's *Squire's Tale* [contained]: "She understood well everything that any fouls may in his leden sayne."

—William Toone's *Etymological Dictionary of Obsolete and Uncommon Words*, 1832

No Need to Learn Greek or Latin

Renowned French philosopher Michel de Montaigne (1533–1592) lampooned imaginary worries writing, "My life has been filled with terrible misfortunes, most of which never happened." He was raised from birth until three years of age among French peasants "in order to bring the boy closer to the common people and and to the conditions of the people who need our help," according to his very wealthy but compassionate father, who hired only servants and tutors who would speak to his son in Latin. Likewise, his father went to great lengths to teach him Greek using conversation, games, and exercises involving meditation, rather than rote memory and drills. Despite his immersion in classical languages, Montaign later downplayed their value, writing: "I must needs acknowledge that the Greek and Latin tongues are great ornaments in a gentleman, but they are purchased at an over-high rate."

George Orwell was also underwhelmed by classical languages, writing in *Politics and the English Language* (1946): "Bad writers, and especially scientific, political, and sociological writers, are nearly always haunted by the notion that Greek or Latin words are grander than Saxon ones."

Flanders-pieces

Pictures that look fair at a distance but coarser near at hand.
—B. E. Gent's *Dictionary of the Termes of the Canting Crew*, c. 1699

Airdrawn, imaginary; drawn or painted in the air.
—William Grimshaw's *Ladies' Lexicon and Parlour Companion*, 1854

A New Approach to Painting

Innovative English painter J. M. W. Turner (1775–1851) was seen by some critics, such as John Ruskin, as an artistic genius for his pre-Impressionist atmospheric effects. But many others considered him a foolish dreamer whose eye for color and technique was suspect. Amazingly, the eccentric and nearly illiterate artist created more than 20,000 works, mostly landscapes, seascapes, and airscapes, which he bequeathed to the English public on his death. When not staying with his patron, Lord Petworth, he lived in various London taverns, including the Ship and Bladebone in Limehouse Reach or in his country home in Twickenham.

Turner, whose remarkably executed early drawings had fetched just a few shillings, was once accused of grossly overcharging buyers for his oil paintings, and he was brought before a magistrate. During the proceedings, the prosecutor sternly asked the middle-aged artist how long it had taken him to create a particular piece of artwork. With a cleverly theatrical display of humility, Turner paused and looked at the judge and replied gently, "All my life, m'lord."

lipopsychy

A swoon; a fainting fit; from Greek *leipo*, to leave, and *psuche*, the soul.

—Rev. John Boag's *Imperial Lexicon of the English Language*, c. 1850

Zoundy, to swoon.

—Walter Skeat's *Glossary of Devonshire Words*, 1896

Music's Second Superstar

Hungarian-born composer and consummate ladies' man Franz Liszt (1811–1886) followed the example set several decades earlier by Italian pianist Niccolò Paganini, giving more than 1,000 concerts between 1839 and 1847. His performance hystrionics included the tossing of his gloves to ecstatic female fans, commonly causing women to faint while witnessing his piano virtuosity and charisma — a charm unsurpassed until Elvis Presley and the Beatles appeared more than a century later.

The French in particular seem to have responded passionately to Liszt's style, perhaps due to a tradition explained by the etymology of the verb "to faint" in William Matthews's *Words: Their Use and Abuse* (1884): "*Faint* is from the French *se feindre*, to pretend, so that originally fainting was a *pretended* weakness or inability. We have an example of the thing originally indicated by the word in the French theaters, where professional fainters are employed, whose business it is to overcome and sink to the floor under the powerful acting of the tragedians."

feuillemorte

A shade of brown of the color of a faded leaf. Anglicised as *feulemort, fillamort, filemot, phillemot,* and *philomot.* French, literally "dead leaf."

—C. A. M. Fennell's *Stanford Dictionary of Anglicised Words and Phrases,* 1892

'Tis the colour of withered leaves falling in Autumn.

—John Locke's *Essay Concerning Humane Understanding,* 1690

Glaucous, a dull or pale green colour passing into greyish blue. *Fuscous,* a dark or sombre hue; dusky, swarthy. [Both] from natural history.

—Sir James Murray's *New English Dictionary,* 1901

Verditure, one of the four green colours chiefly used by painters.

—John Kersey's *New English Dictionary,* 1772

Faded Colors

Alice Earle's *Customs and Fashions in Old New England* (1893) included these old-fashioned colors from 1668: "*gridolin* (*gris-de-lin,* or flax blossom), *grain color* (scarlet), *Kendal green, watchet blue* [light blue], *barry, milly, tuly* [deep red, like tuly silk], *stamel red, Bristol red* [still known in Britain], 'sad color,' . . . [all of] whose signification and identification was lost with the death of the century. In later days, *Congress brown, Federal blue,* and *Independence green* show our new nation."

Crime and
Punishment

Compromise is the best and cheapest lawyer.

—Robert Louis Stevenson (1850–1894), Scottish novelist

wrawling

Quarreling or contending with a loud voice. *Raising a wraw* is exciting a quarrel and confusion in the streets. [From] *wrawe*, angry.

> —Robert Willan's *Glossary of the West Riding of Yorkshire*, 1814

Witnessfully, that which can be fully proved by many witnesses.

> —Charles Mackay's *Lost Beauties of the English Language*, 1874

Insult But No Injury

Alice Morse Earle's *Colonial Days in Old New York* (1896) informed readers that two and three centuries ago, New York attorneys were inclined to litigate over colorful, now-forgotten insults: "Suits for defamation were frequent, through opprobrious name-calling, and on very slight though irritating grounds. It would certainly seem a rather disproportionate amount of trouble to bring a lawsuit simply because you were called a *black pudding* [a sausage], a *verklikker*, or tale-bearer, or even a Turk, though of course no one would stand being called a *horned beast* or a *hay thief*. Nor was

thou swine an offensive term too petty to be passed over in silence. The terrible epithets *spitter-baard*, a beard with saliva in it and *Dutch dough-face* seem to make a climax of opprobriousness, but the word *moff* was worse, for it was the despised term applied in Holland to the Germans, and it led to a quarrel with knives."

tybert

A [medieval and Renaissance] name for a cat. Shakespeare considers Tybalt as the same; whence some of the insulting jests of Mercutio, who called Tybalt "rat catcher" and "king of cats" [in] *Romeo and Juliet*.

—Robert Nares's *Glossary of the Works of English Authors*, 1859

The Defense Rests

In 1521 French lawyer Bartholomew Chassenée honed his legal skills by defending his most unusual clients — rats that had ravaged a barley crop earlier that year. In Autun, France, the farmers were out for revenge, but not surprisingly the "defendants" failed to appear, prompting Chassanée to argue that the summons was invalid because it failed to have been served on all the rats. After another summons was issued, Chassenée pleaded cleverly that "evilly-disposed cats" owned by the prosecutors had kept his clients from appearing through intimidation, for which he demanded a bond guaranteeing the rats safe passage to court. When prosecutors refused to provide such an assurance the judge had no choice but to dismiss the absurd charges.

The first recorded animal trial took place in 864 — that of a hive of bees that had severely stung a man. These cases continued for more than a thousand years, involving horses, dogs, chickens, and even caterpillars and gnats. A 1993 film titled *The Advocate* involved a famous prosecution of a pig.

cucking-stool

A chair in which an offender was placed to be hooted at or pelted by the mob; or it might be used for ducking its occupant; from Icelandic *kukr*, dung.

—Charles Annandale's *Dictionary of the English Language*, 1897

An instrument of punishment formerly in use for scolds, disorderly women, fraudulent tradespeople, etc.

—Sir James Murray's *New English Dictionary*, 1893

Farewell to the Cucking-Stool

The last recorded use of the cucking-stool (shown below) took place in 1745, in Kingston, Surrey. The English antiquary William Cole (1714–1782), writing around 1780, recalled how this device was used: "When I was a boy and lived . . . in the great corner house at the bridge-foot next to Magdalan College, Cambridge, I remember to have seen a woman ducked for scolding. The chair hung by a pulley fastened to a beam about the middle of the bridge; and the woman having been fastened in the chair, she was let under the water three times successively, and then taken out. On the back panel of [the stool] was an engraving representing devils laying hold of scolds."

Robert Chambers's *Book of Days* (1864) added, "That the 'cold water cure' had a wholesome effect upon the tongues of not a few of the fair sex is agreed on by all old writers who mention the subject, poets as well as prosaists."

autum-divers

Pickpockets who practise in churches. [From] *autum*, a church, and *diver*, a pickpocket.

—George Matsell's *Vocabulum, or the Rogue's Lexicon*, 1859

The Roots of *Mack the Knife*

One of England's most notorious thieves and disguise artists was named Mary Young (c. 1700–1740), aka Jenny Diver. Her most imaginative crime was, according to the *Newgate Chronicle*, to attach two artificial arms to a carefully designed costume, artfully padded to simulate pregnancy. Finely dressed in this outfit, she and several accomplices would attend church services, seating themselves among the well-to-do. Jenny would wait patiently for victims to hunch forward in prayer before helping herself to the watches and other valuables in their pockets, which she passed to a cohort, her clasped "hands" and pregnant appearance serving to disarm nearby parishioners. But she was caught twice by 1738 and transported to Virginia, from which she returned home illegally. She was hanged after this third offense, but achieved a measure of immortality.

John Gay included her among Capt. Macheath's entourage of lowlife characters in *The Beggar's Opera* in 1728, a production updated after two centuries by Kurt Weill's *The Threepenny Opera* in 1928. Even later, Jenny was mentioned in the pop song "Mack the Knife," along with her underworld colleagues Macheath, Sukey Tawdry, and Lucy Brown.

gantelope

This punishment, which is called *running the gauntlet*, is seldom inflicted except for crimes as will excite a general antipathy amongst the seamen, as on some occasions the culprit would pass without receiving a single blow, particularly in cases of mutiny or sedition.

—William Falconer's *Universal Dictionary of the Marine*, 1771

Mutiny on the Bounty

In 1789, Fletcher Christian assumed command of the ill-fated H.M.S. *Bounty* by casting Capt. William Bligh and eighteen loyalists adrift in the South Pacific in the most famous maritime mutiny ever staged. "Breadfruit Bligh," as crewmembers called him, wanted to circumnavigate the globe on his return voyage from Tahiti via the dangerous route around the southern horn of Africa, which added to the tension between the crew and himself.

Christian eventually established a colony on the two-square-mile outcropping called Pitcairn Island, which is today inhabited by his descendants, those of crewmen and their Tahitian wives, and some newcomers. After managing to sail back to civilization, Bligh was appointed governor of New South Wales, Australia in 1806 despite lingering doubts by superiors about his interpersonal skills. But he was relieved of his command in 1808 after being revolted against twice by unhappy colonists and military officers alike.

darkmans

The night.

—Capt. Alexander Smith's *A Complete History of the Lives and Robberies of the Most Notorious Highwaymen, Footpads, Shoplifts & Cheats of Both Sexes*, 1719

The Life and Death of Cartouche

Born Louis Dominique Garthausen in 1693 to a German wine merchant, he later called himself Cartouche to cloak his identity. He became a popular hero to the French lower classes, and is even saluted as an early influence on the French Revolution. His gangs targeted the route between Paris and Versailles, where they relieved aristocrats of their valuables and, like Robin Hood, distributed some of his booty to the poor. This legendary highwayman — the subject of a 1962 movie, starring Jean-Paul Belmondo in the title role — was broken of his egalitarian ways on the wheel and executed on this date in 1721.

He once came across a suicidal man who claimed to owe a threatening debt collector more than he could ever repay. Cartouche agreed to pay the debt if the man joined him. So the man agreed to invite the surprised debt collector to meet him one evening for this transaction at a quiet location. There the money was exchanged, a receipt issued, and the debt forgiven. But after the two shook hands and parted, some of Cartouche's men stepped from the shrubbery and took back the money, enriching Cartouche's reputation as a defender of the downtrodden.

ambidexter

He that useth his left hand as well as his right, that plays on both sides. But in the legal acception it signifies that juror or embraceor who takes money on both sides for giving his verdict.

—Thomas Blount's *Law Dictionary and Glossary*, 1717

Testiculouse, of high generative power. In ancient times, a man gave *testimony* while placing his hands between the thighs, as though swearing by his generative powers.

—Joseph Shipley's *Dictionary of Early English*, 1955

Michaelmas Day

The Lawless Court is kept at King's Hill, about half a mile northeast of Rochford Church. . . . Here the tenants kneel and do their homage. The time is the Wednesday morning next after Michaelmas Day upon the first cock-crowing, without any kind of light but such as the heavens will offer. They are all to whisper to each other. . . . He that owes suit and service thereto and appears not, forfeits to the lord double his rent every hour he is absent. A tenant of this manor forfeited not long ago his land for non-attendance but was restored to it, the lord only taking a fine. The court is called "Lawless" because [it was] held at an unlawful hour.

—Philip Morant's *The History and Antiquities of Essex*, 1768

yesterfang

That which was taken, captured, or caught on the day preceding.

—Edward Lloyd's *Encyclopædic Dictionary*, 1895

Stockholm Syndrome

In 1973, a botched robbery of the Stockholm bank Kreditbanken resulted in two men holding four bank employees hostage in the vault for five days. Local police used several tactics to force a surrender, including drilling a hole in the safe and threatening to pump in noxious gas, which was done. After their release, the hostages admitted that they were far more afraid of the police than of their abductors, leading psychologists to study this and other related events and name it Stockholm Syndrome.

Stockholm Syndrome is considered an important ingredient of the early type of union known as "marriage by capture," in which a young man would kidnap a girl from a neighboring village — sometimes with the help of a friend, who served as the forerunner of the "best man" we know today. The groom would then hide out for several weeks or a month (corresponding to the modern "honeymoon") with his abducted bride, during which time she often developed affection for him, and if so, the couple would return to her village for her father's blessing. Military "boot camp" training and fraternity hazing are two other modern activities that involve Stockholm Syndrome.

faleste

A capital punishment inflicted on a malefactor on the seashore by laying him bound on the sands till the next full tide carried him away. From Norman *falese*, sands, rocks, cliffs.

—John Bouvier's *Law Dictionary*, 1839

Bloodworthy, deserving of blood, in the sense of capital punishment.

—Edward Lloyd's *Encyclopædic Dictionary*, 1895

Britain's Hanging Offenses

In medieval times, eating meat on one of the almost 200 "lean days," when meat was forbidden, could be prosecuted as a hanging offense. In the 1700s, English citizens — some under ten — were commonly executed for petty theft. Other capital crimes were livestock rustling, forgery, "sacrilege," sodomy, "unauthorized tree-felling," postal theft, "blacking the face or using a disguise whilst committing a crime," poaching, "being in the company of Gypsies for one month," petty larceny, damaging bridges or industrial equipment and even begging.

In fact, by 1810, Britain's "Bloody Code" included about 220 capital crimes. Historian John Stow (c. 1525–1605) estimated that 72,000 people were hanged in Britain during Henry VIII's reign — more than

five per day, when England had less than five million people. A few mostly military crimes, such as treason, "piracy with violence," and "giving false air signals" remained subject to the death penalty until 1998, when Britain finally outlawed this practice.

deodand

Formerly, in English Law, from the earliest times, a personal chattel which had been the immediate occasion of the death of a rational creature, and for that reason given to God — that is, forfeited to the king. . . . The pious object of the forfeiture was early lost sight of, and the king might, and often did, cede his rights to deodands.

—William Whitney's *Century Dictionary*, 1889

Let the Punishment Fit the Crime

In 1846, the deodand was formally outlawed by Britain's parliament. From the Latin *Deo dandum*, "that given to God," this legal term was based on the Church's doctrine of purgatory, prescribing how to administer some cases involving injury and death. Sir Henry Finch's *Law* (1613) stated: "If a man being upon a cart carrying faggots . . . fall down by the moving of one of the horses in the cart and die of it, both that and all the other horses in [pulling] the cart, and the cart itself, are forfeit. And these are called *deodands*." Originally, the king confiscated the animal, or even inanimate property, such as a boat or a ladder, that was determined to have caused an injury. During medieval times, animals including bees, gnats, chickens, rodents and pigs were tried for crimes according to the laws applied to people. Even plagues and natural disasters were sometimes blamed on animals, which were prosecuted accordingly.

gullantine

To kill, destroy. Evidently from *guillotine*.
—Thomas Darlington's *The Folk-Speech of South Cheshire*, 1887

Off With Their Heads

Dr. Joseph Ignace Guillotin, an avid egalitarian, felt that capital punishment should be administered without regard to wealth or social position. In the late 18th century, privileged folks were often beheaded, but the poor were generally hanged. While the results were about the same, hanging and the ax involved a greater risk of gruesome mishap than did its high-tech cousin. Guillotin's lobbying efforts prompted others to develop what became known as the "philanthropic decapitation machine," which was first tested on bales of hay, then sheep and corpses, and finally on a highwayman in 1792. The good doctor asserted that it performed its task "in a twinkling," and promised that the condemned would feel nothing but a sense of "refreshing coolness" — a theory he was never able to prove.

But this device was not the first of its kind. In fact, William the Conqueror introduced "lightheadedness" into Britain in 1076. Another of the guillotine's forerunners, the "Halifax Gibbet," was first employed in Halifax, England, in 1286. Its use included a sense of sport, allowing the condemned a chance to withdraw his or her head and escape on foot beyond the parish border a mile away, provided her or she would accept lifetime exile.

drunk as a fiddler

Exceedingly drunk. The intemperance of professional fiddlers at evening parties was proverbial; . . . also *drunk as a cobbler*. From as early as the 15th century in England, cobblers were proverbial for drunkenness.

—Albert Hyamson's *Dictionary of English Phrases*, 1922

The Drunkard's Cloak

Before temperance societies and Alcoholics Anonymous were established to offer alternatives to habitual drinking, drunkenness was rampant in Britain and America. Some towns imposed much harsher sanctions, such as one called a "drunkard's cloak" in Richard Heslop's *Glossary of Northumberland* (1894): "A tub with holes in the sides for the arms to pass through, the head appearing through a hole made in the end, which rested on the shoulders. In former times used in Newcastle for the punishment of drunkards and others, who were led through the streets in this strange guise."

John Brand's *History and Antiquities of Newcastle* (1789) added: "In the time of the Commonwealth, it appears that the magistrates of Newcastle upon Tyne punished scolds with the branks, and drunkards by making them carry a tub, called the *drunkard's cloak*, through the streets of that town. We shall presume that there is no longer any occasion for the former, but why has the latter been laid aside?"

wooden hills

A common slang term for stairs.

—Thomas Darlington's *The Folk-Speech of South Cheshire,* 1887

England's Prison Discipline Society

followed the lead of Philadelphia's Society for Assisting Distressed Prisoners (1776), as well as the findings of English reformer John Howard, who had toured Europe's prisons and found them woefully inept. Joseph Haydn's *Dictionary of Dates* (1841) described the society's mission as "the employment of prisoners and the prevention of crime by inspiring a dread of punishment, and by inducing the criminal, on his discharge from confinement, to abandon his vicious pursuits." This well-intentioned group helped establish the use of such devices as the "treadmill," an innocuous-sounding piece of prison hardware (depicted below) intended to exhaust and demoralize feisty inmates — and hopefully induce their overdue repentance — without performing any useful work.

But the treadmill was found to provoke physical injury and a host of unwelcome psychological problems, including anger, resentment and

depression, and this social experiment was abandoned near the turn of the century. Its name, now synonymous with monotony, was later transferred to a piece of gym equipment used for horizontal walking. Ironically, the original treadmill was redesigned in miniature for use in gyms, under the familiar and euphemistic brand name, Stairmaster.

blasphematour

A blasphemer; from French *blasphémateur.*
Blasphemeress, a woman who blasphemes; from Old
French *blasphemeresse. Blasphement*, blasphemy.

—Sir James Murray's *New English Dictionary*, 1888

Legal Convictions for Blasphemy

Joseph Haydn's *Dictionary of Dates* (1841) chronicled the history
of English blasphematours until fairly recent times: "Daniel Isaac
Eaton was tried and convicted in London of blasphemy, 13th March,
1812. A protestant clergyman, named Robert Taylor, was tried in
London twice for the same crime, and as often convicted. Taylor was
last brought to the bar and sentenced to two years' imprisonment,
and largely fined, for . . . reviling the Redeemer in his discourses,
July 1831. Even as late as December 1840, two prosecutions against
publishers of blasphemous writings subjected the offenders to
[punishment]."

Britain's Blasphemy Act of 1698 stipulated
that for denying the Holy Trinity, a person
could be prevented from holding public office
and receiving some inheritances. Until 1925,
blasphemy charges were brought against
Britons, not only for expressing contempt for
God and the Scriptures — for which fines,
imprisonment and even corporal punishment
were enforced — but also for insulting high-
ranking government officials. The last prison
sentence for blasphemy was handed down to a
Speakers' Corner orator in 1921.

Customs, Traditions and Superstitions

Such is the way of all superstition — whether in astrology, dreams, omens, divine judgments or the like — wherein men, having a delight in such vanities, mark the events where they are fulfilled; but where they fail, though this happen much oftener, [they] pass them by.

—Francis Bacon's *Novum Organum*, 1620

callithumpian

A band of discordant instruments; a member.

—William Craigie's *Dictionary of American English*, 1940

An allusion to [Greek poetry muse] Calliope, as well as to thumping.

—John Bartlett's *Dictionary of Americanisms*, 1884

The Butcher's Serenade of London

Robert Chambers's *Book of Days* (1864) described the 18th-century "butcher's serenade," a discarded English marriage custom at London's Clare Market, near The Strand: "The performers were the butcher's men, the bonny boys that wear the sleeves of blue. A set of these lads, having duly accomplished themselves for the purpose, made a point of attending in front of a house containing a marriage party with their cleavers [struck with bones] wherewith to perform a sort of rude serenade.

"Sometimes the group would consist of four, the cleaver of each ground to the production of a certain note. But a full band, one entitled to the highest grade of reward, would not be less than eight, producing a complete octave, and where there was a fair skill, this series of notes would have all the fine effect of a peal of bells. . . . The cleaver *epithalamium* [a congratulatory nuptial song] seldom failed to diffuse a good humour throughout the neighbourhood, and one cannot but regret that it is rapidly passing among the things that were."

elf-locks

Locks so clotted together were supposed to be the operation of fairies; a superstition [found in] *Romeo & Juliet.*

— Rev. Alexander Dyce's *Glossary to the Works of Shakespeare*, 1902

Ascension Day Superstitions

Occurring 39 days after Easter, this holiday inspired many strange beliefs in Britain. A. R. Wright's *British Calendar Customs* (1936) mentioned one: "Another protection against fire and other calamities is believed, in Nottinghamshire, to be an egg laid on Ascension Day and placed on the roof of a house." According to the English Folklore Society, in Eccleshall, Staffordshire, "a piece of hawthorne gathered on Ascension Day is the proper [charm against lightning]. It must be brought to you, not gathered on your own ground."

Charlotte Burne's *Shropshire Folk-Lore: A Sheaf of Gleanings* (1883) suggested, "Rain which falls on Ascension Day is a favorite remedy for bad eyes, and Good Friday bread is supposed to keep good for years." But *Notes & Queries* (1886) cautioned that in Wales, "The whole of Lord Penrhyn's slate quarrymen [one shown here] took a holiday on Ascension Day because of the universally prevalent superstition that a fatal accident will inevitably cut off those who work during that day. This strange superstition is common among the thousands of quarrymen engaged in North Wales."

drent

Drowned; from Scottish *drencean*.

—William Toone's *Etymological Dictionary of Obsolete and Uncommon Words*, 1832

Sillyhow, the membrane that covers the head of the foetus. Perhaps from *selig*, happy, and *heft*, head.

—Samuel Johnson's *Dictionary of the English Language*, 1755

The Lucky Caul

William Henderson's *Notes on the Folk-lore of the Northern Counties of England and the Borders* (1879) described the the use of a small piece of human placenta as a good-luck charm: "Children born with a *hallihoo* — a *holy*, or fortunate, *hood*, or *caul* — around their heads are deemed lucky, but the caul must be preserved carefully, for should it be lost or thrown away, the child will pine away or die. This superstition however is worldwide and of such antiquity as to be reproved by St. Chrysostom in several of his homilies."

Henderson continued, "Seamen used to purchase cauls to save them from drowning; advocates [attorneys] likewise that they might thereby be imbued with eloquence. Twenty guineas were asked for one in 1779, £12 in 1813, six guineas in 1848. In this last case, the caul was of some antiquity and £15 had originally been given for it by a seaman who carried it with him for thirty years." To ensure there would be no need for one's ghost to return to claim his *hallihoo* after death, people once insisted on having this birth remnant buried with them.

Friday-face

A grave or gloomy expression; [also] *Friday-faced, Friday-look.*

—Sir James Murray's *New English Dictionary*, 1901

Friday Superstitions

Fridays have long been regarded as a day when bad things could happen. Since the Middle Ages, hangings generally took place on Fridays in England and America, and weddings were avoided. Friday was named for the Nordic fertility goddess, Frigga, who was upon the advent of Christianity branded a witch because of her unabashed pagan nature and removed from the pantheon. As revenge, she was thought to conjure up bad luck on Fridays. This day, on which Eve reportedly tempted Adam, was also considered the unluckiest day for ships to sail. As late as 1933, A. G. Street's *Country Days* mentioned a practice reflecting deep-seated reservations about this day: "My father once decided to start harvest on a Friday, and the men went out on a Thursday evening and, unpaid, cut along one side of the first field with their scythes in order to dodge the malign fate which a Friday start would begin."

Elsewhere, John Harland's *Lancashire Folklore* (1867) reported: "Amongst other popular superstitions . . . a man must never go a-courting on a Friday. If an unlucky fellow is caught with lady-love on that day, he is followed home by a band of musicians playing on pokers, tongs, pan-lids, &c., unless he can rid himself of his tormentors by giving them money for drink."

deathwatch

The [ticking] sound produced by some small species of insects, which live in old wood, when they strike their horny heads against the wood calling their companions.

—James Barclay's *Dictionary of the English Language*, 1848

The sound produced is, by the superstitious, thought to be a forewarning of death.

—Robert Hunter's *Encyclopædic Dictionary*, 1894

I have since, nearly three years ago, oft found by trial, that it is a noise upon paper by a little nimble running worm, just like a louse.

—Richard Baxter's *The Certainty of the World of Spirits Fully Evinced*, 1691

The Mysterious Groaning Board

Edmund King's *Ten Thousand Wonderful Things* (c. 1853) described a short-lived curiosity found in English pubs which was discovered during Charles II's second reign: "Groaning boards were the wonder in London in 1682. An elm plank was exhibited to the king which, being touched by a hot iron, invariably produced a sound resembling deep groans. At the Bowman tavern in Drury Lane, the mantelpiece did the same so well that it was supposed to be part of the same elm tree. And the dresser at the Queen's Arm Tavern, [at] St. Martin le Grand, was found to possess the same quality. Strange times when such things were deemed wonderful, even to meriting exhibition before the monarch."

laver

To wash. It was anciently [in the 13th century] the custom for guests to wash before sitting down to meals, and it seems that the signal for this ablution was given by sounding a trumpet.

—William Toone's *Etymological Dictionary of Obsolete and Uncommon Words*, 1832

Miners' Superstitions

Christina Hole's *English Folklore* (1940) mentioned several miners' superstitions that survived well into the 20th century: "The older men in South Wales have a great dislike for washing their backs; they say that to do so will cause the mine roof to fall on top of them. In the East Midlands they say that accidents are most frequent when the broad beans are in bloom."

Sir Charles Igglesden's *Those Superstitions* (1931) added: "The miner refrains from washing his back in the belief that it reduces his strength. A miner has a great fear of being 'weak-backed,' and it is told of the Lancashire miners of forty years ago that for this reason they never washed their bodies, but merely their hands, forearms, face, and neck. With the advent of new houses and the consequent installation of baths they have dropped this superstition to a large extent. Many miners have to go to work during the very early hours of the morning. If a man happens to meet a woman on his way to work at such a time he considers it very unlucky."

sanglier

If it should be demanded what you will call a boar of three years old, you may answer, "He is a young boar which hath lately left the sounder." An old boar you must call a *singular*, or *singlier*, that hath left the sounder four or five years since.

—Nicholas Cox's *The Gentleman's Recreation*, 1697

Brimming, a sow, when she takes the boar, is said to be *a-brimming*, and the boar is said to *brim* her.

—William Marshall's *Provincialisms of East Yorkshire*, 1788

Bringing in the Boar's Head

In medieval England it was customary to commence all great Christmas feasts by the solemn ceremony of "Bringing in the Boar's Head" as the initial dish. The master-cook, preceded by the trumpeters and other musicians, followed by huntsmen with boar-spears and drawn falchions and pages carrying mustard, bore the smoking head aloft on a silver platter, which he deposited at the head of the table. The head was garnished and garlanded with rosemary and laurel, and a lemon was placed between its grinning chops. . . . The custom goes back to pre-Christian days. The Druids killed a boar at the winter solstice, and offered its head in sacrifice to Freyda, the goddess of peace and plenty, who was supposed to ride upon a boar with golden bristles.

—William Walsh's *Curiosities of Popular Customs*, 1897

deterge

To wash off or out; chiefly in medical use, to clean away foul or offensive matter from the body. Hence, *deterging, deterger, detergent, detersion. Detergency,* detergent quality; cleansing power. Also, the process of cleansing a solid by means of a liquid.

—Sir James Murray's *New English Dictionary,* 1897

Sweetening Saturday

The first Saturday of June was an annual bathing day for some rural families in the British Isles into the 19th century. In *Those Superstitions* (1931) Charles Igglesden noted: "If two people wash in the same water at the same time it brings bad luck. During the [First World] War, when water was scarce, the risk was frequently taken, but not without leading to heated altercations between those who believed in the superstition and those who did not. An amusing incident was related to me by a sergeant. The battalion had just come out of the front line and the chance of a wash was possible in the cellars of a cluster of houses. Men cleansed themselves as best they could, but presently there was a heated dispute between two lads, one of whom had the audacity to start washing from the same water as the other. 'You'll bring bad luck to me, will you?' A blow was struck. It led to a scuffle, and the two combatants were hustled out of the cellar by their comrades."

At one time, many Bulgarian peasant women bathed only once — just before their weddings — and devout Spanish women only with the permission of their confessors.

egg-wife-trot

An easy jog, such a speed as farmers' wives carry their eggs to the market.

—William Carr's *Dialect of Craven*, 1828

Good Friday Customs

According to William Henderson's *Notes on the Folk-lore of the Northern Counties of England and the Borders* (1879), "In Suffolk, eggs laid on Good Friday are kept with the greatest care by the farmers' wives, who maintain that they will never go bad, and that a piece of such an egg gives immediate relief to a person suffering from colic." Henderson also recalled hearing "from a clergyman familiar with the North Riding of Yorkshire that great care is there taken not to disturb the earth in any way; it were impious to use spade, plough, or harrow. He remembers, when a boy, hearing of a villager . . . who shocked his neighbours by planting potatoes on Good Friday — but they never came up."

The reason for this was found in John Campbell's *Witchcraft and Second Sight in the Highlands* (1902): "There was hardly any

 belief that had a stronger hold on the Highlander's mind than that on no account should iron be put into the ground on this day. So great was the aversion of doing so that the more superstitious extended the prohibition to every Friday. . . . If a burial was to take place, the grave was opened on the previous day and the earth was settled over the coffin with a wooden shovel."

tocher

A word principally applied to the fortune of persons in the middle and lower ranks of life who are too poor to give their daughters doweries. A *tocher* stands in about the same relation to a dowery as a house does to a mansion.

—Charles Mackay's *Lost Beauties of the English Language*, 1874

The Legend of St. Nicholas

The myth of this fourth-century patron of gift-givers — known as Santa Claus — grew out of his benevolence toward a penniless man who could not afford dowries for his three daughters and felt compelled to sell them into prostitution. Nicholas was said to have tossed a bag of gold pieces through the father's window on three consecutive nights, which allowed the daughters to find suitable husbands. These small sacks became the three gold balls traditionally used as a symbol by pawnbrokers.

In some English cathedrals, a Christmas "boy-bishop," which represented Nicholas as a pious boy, reigned from December 6 until Innocent's Day on December 28th. This medieval office served as a source of levity to the congregations partly due to its solemn intent. It was dissolved by Henry VIII, but continued on the Continent for two more centuries. In England the boy-bishop was revived at Salisbury and Hereford cathedrals, and in some smaller churches in reduced form beginning in the 1950s. A boy-bishop was even entombed in Salisbury Cathedral after dying there "in office".

rorid

Dewy.
　—Noah Webster's *American Dictionary of the English Language*, 1828

Rorigenous, produced of dew. *Rorifluous*, flowing with dew; adaptation of Latin *rorifluus*.
　—Nathaniel Bailey's *Etymological English Dictionary*, 1749

May-dew, dew of May, supposed to have the property of whitening linen, of preserving beauty, and of affording a red odiferous spirit by distillation.
　—T. Ellwood Zell's *Encyclopedia of Knowledge and Language*, 1871

Collecting May Dew

In Edinburgh's *Arthur's Seat*, and throughout the British Isles, girls and even grown women carefully gathered *May-dew* from grass and plant leaves as late as the 1930s. Wielding sponges, flat scraping tools and tiny reservoirs at dawn during the month of May, they did so in order to partake of dew's renowned cosmetic virtues. Even the well-educated were once convinced of its properties, as Samuel Pepys revealed in his diary entry for May 28, 1667: "After dinner, my wife away down with Jane and W. Hewer to Woolwich, in order to [get] a little ayre, and to lie there tonight, and so to gather May-dew tomorrow morning, which Mrs. Turner hath taught her is the only thing in the world to wash her face with; and I am contented with it."

Gabriel's hounds

These phantom hounds, jet black and breathing flames, frequent bleak and dreary moors on tempestuous nights, and woe betide the unlucky wretch who chances to cross their path.

—Elizabeth M. Wright's *Rustic Speech and Folklore*, 1914

At Wednesbury, the colliers going to their pits early in the morning hear the noise of a "pack of hounds" in the air, to which they give the name *Gabriel's hounds*, though the more sober and judicious take them only to be wild geese making this noise in their flight.

—White Kennett's *Lansdowne Manuscript of Provincial Words*, c. 1700

Evil Spirits Unleashed

Reginald Scot's *Discovery of Witchcraft* (1584) commented on these fears: "[They] have so frayed us with bull-beggars, witches, urchins, elves, hags, satyrs, pans, faunes, sylvans, the *spoorney*, nymphs, changelings, *incubus*, the *Man in the Oke*, the *hell-waine* [wagon], and such other bugbears, that we were afraid of our own shadowes." Scot also offered "a charm to find who hath bewitched your cattle," recommending that farmers "put a pair of breeches upon the cow's head and beat her out of the pasture with a good cudgel upon a Friday and she will run right to the witch's door and strike thereat with her horns."

telling the bees

Probably no superstition is so widely held in country areas, even today, as "telling the bees." As soon as the master or mistress had breathed the last, a member of the household visited the hives and . . . said, "Little brownies, your master is dead." Silence was then observed for a few moments. If the bees then began to hum, it was a sign that they consented to remain under the new owner.

—Edwin and Mona Radford's *Encyclopædia of Superstitions*, 1949

Keeping Bees Happy

Sidney Addy's *Household Tales with Other Traditional Remains* (1895) added this to the above-mentioned custom, which may date from ancient Greek times: "Tins containing funeral biscuits soaked in wine are put in front of the hives so that the bees may partake of their master's funeral feast. Two kinds of funeral cakes are used — namely biscuits and 'burying-cakes,' the latter being given only to the poor. At Eyam in Derbyshire, a portion of the 'burnt drink' and of the three-cornered cakes used at funerals is given to the bees of the deceased

beekeeper. Sometimes pieces of black crepe are pinned upon the hives. It is said that bees must be told of their master's death or they will all die." Charles Igglesden's *Those Superstitions* (1931) added this 1860s Kentish custom: "The herdsmen at once went to the cattle and sheep and whispered to them that their old master was dead. It was explained that had the farmhands neglected to carry out this duty the [animals] would have suddenly died."

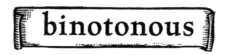

binotonous

Consisting of two notes; [companion word of] *monotonous*.

—Rev. John Boag's *Imperial Lexicon of the English Language*, c. 1850

Cuckoos Begin to Announce Spring in Britain

The cuckoo was looked upon as the embodiment of spring in early times, and the weather was supposed to change as soon as it appeared. At Towednack [Cornwall] there is a legend that an old man once threw a hollow log on his fire one wintry April day. A cuckoo flew out of it, and at once the weather became warm and spring-like. The tale is still commemorated in a local holiday called Cuckoo Feast, which is held in late April. In Sussex the bird is said to be released by the old woman who has charge of all cuckoos in mid-April at Heathfield Cuckoo Fair.

It is lucky to hear it for the first time when you have money in your pocket. Whatever you are doing on that occasion will be your principal occupation during the year. Hence it is very unlucky to hear it first when fasting or in bed, as this means hunger or illness. If the first call comes from the right or from in front, it is a good omen; in Wales, you will prosper if you are standing on grass, but to hear it on stony or barren ground means a year. In some districts it was formerly the custom to roll on the grass as soon as the first note was heard.

—Eleanor Hull's *Folklore of the British Isles*, 1928

Holidays, Festivals and Observances

A lovely thing about Christmas is that it's compulsory, like a thunderstorm, and we all go through it together.

—Garrison Keillor, writer and creator of *A Prairie Home Companion*

gruffins

Used of a cow who, when she lifts her back, is said to
"hump her *gruffins*."

—Thomas Darlington's *The Folk-Speech of South Cheshire*, 1887

Lifting Monday

Peter Roberts's *Cambrian Popular Antiquities* (1815) reported: "On
Easter Monday and Tuesday, a ceremony takes place among the lower
orders in North Wales. It is called *lifting*, and consists in lifting
a person in a chair [shown here] three times from the ground. On
Monday, the men lift the women, and on Tuesday the women lift the
men. The lifters go in troops and, with a permitted freedom, seize
the person they intend to lift and, having persuaded him or her to sit
on the chair, lift whoever it is three times with cheering, and then
require a small compliment [tip]. A little resistance, real or affected,
creates no small merriment; much resistance would excite contempt
and perhaps indignation."

Charles Hardwick commented on "heaving," as it was also called in
his *Traditions, Superstitions, and Folklore Chiefly [in] Lancashire
and the North of England* (1872): "It was commonly performed in
the public streets and caused much amusement. But it was a rude

and indelicate piece of practical joking
... originally intended to typify the
Resurrection of Christ." According
to George Long's *Folklore Calendar*
(1930), heaving was done to King
Edward I (1239–1307) on Easter Monday
"by a party of lively maids of honor."

quignogs

Ridiculous fancies or conceits; Cornwall.

—Joseph Wright's *English Dialect Dictionary*, 1898–1905

"You're full of *quignogs.*"

—Frederick W. P. Jago's *The Ancient Language and the Dialect of Cornwall*, 1882

The Feast of Fools

T. Ellwood Zell's *Encyclopedia of Knowledge and Language* (1871) reported that the Feast of Fools was celebrated on about December 28 "with the most absurd ceremonies, both by clergy and the laity in several countries in Europe, from the fifth to the sixteenth century. At first, only the boys of the choir and young sacristans played the principle part in them, while the bishops and other clergy formed part of the audience. *A Bishop of Unreason* was appointed, the forms and ceremonies of the Church were travestied, indecent songs were sung . . . and all manners of fooleries enacted. The ass often played an important part in the proceedings, being sometimes led towards the altar, having hymns sung in its honor."

Ebenezer Brewer's *Dictionary of Phrase and Fable* (1898) offered this detail: "The mass was burlesqued, and braying often took the place of customary responses. Obscene jests and dances were common. . . . An ass formed an essential feature and, from time to time, the whole procession imitated the braying of this animal, especially in the place of *Amen.*" The Feast of Fools was finally banned in 1431, but continued to take place in modified forms in France as late as 1644.

lamb's-wool

A favorite liquor among the common people [consumed traditionally during the Christmas holidays and on New Year's Eve] composed of ale and roasted apples. The pulp of the roasted apple [was] worked up with the ale till the mixture formed a smooth beverage. Fanciful etymologies for this popular word have been thought of, but it was probably named from its smoothness, resembling the wool of lambs.

—Robert Nares's *Glossary of the Works of English Authors*, 1859

The pulpe of the roasted apples, in number, foure or five, according to the greatnesse of the apples, mixed in a quart of faire water, laboured together untill it come to be as apples and ale, which we call *lambes-wooll.*

—Thomas Johnson's *Herbal*, 1633

Holiday Cheer

Charles Hardwick's *Traditions, Superstitions, and Folklore Chiefly [in] Lancashire and the North of England* (1872) explained, "Young women went about with a wassail bowl of

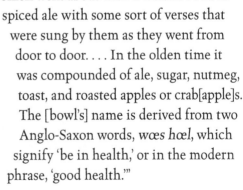

spiced ale with some sort of verses that were sung by them as they went from door to door. . . . In the olden time it was compounded of ale, sugar, nutmeg, toast, and roasted apples or crab[apple]s. The [bowl's] name is derived from two Anglo-Saxon words, *wœs hœl*, which signify 'be in health,' or in the modern phrase, 'good health.'"

algerining

Prowling about with intent to rob. Often said of a tramp.
A very curious word. Its derivation from the Algiers pirates
is self-evident.

—Edgerton Leigh's *Glossary of Words Used in Cheshire*, 1877

From *Algerine*, an inhabitant of Algiers. The greatest
commerce of the Algerines consists in . . . piratical plunder
all over the Mediterranean.

—Joseph Wright's *English Dialect Dictionary*, 1898–1905

Kenning glass, an old name for a telescope. *Lookstick*, a
telescope.

—Frank Bowen's *Sea Slang: The Old-Timers' Expressions*, 1929

Old Greenwich Fair

If Whit Monday dawned brightly, every street in London showed, from
an early hour, streams of lads and lasses pouring towards . . . Greenwich,
five miles off. No railway then, no steamers on the river; their place
was supplied by stagecoaches and wherries. When
the holiday-maker and his partner had, by whatever
means, made their way to Greenwich, they found
the principal street filled . . . with shows, theatrical
booths, and stalls. . . . One of the old pensioners
. . . would be drawing halfpence for the use of
his telescope, whereby you could see St. Paul's
Cathedral or the pirates hanging in chains along
the river — the last a favorite spectacle.

—Robert Chambers's *Book of Days*, 1864

flutter the dovecots

To cause a mild excitement in society; Shakespeare's *Coriolanus*.

—Albert Hyamson's *Dictionary of English Phrases*, 1922

The First Shakespeare Festival Fizzles

Robert Chambers's *Book of Days* (1864) reported on an event which is commonplace today: "On September 6, 1769, and two following days, Stratford-upon-Avon witnessed a succession of festivities such as seldom befall an English country town. The object of these remarkable doings was the commemoration of the great Shakespeare, whose remains, upwards of a 150 years before, had been deposited in the chancel of the parish church of this, his native place."

Despite Chambers's salute, this "bicentennial," organized by impresario David Garrick, was in fact five years late and not held during April, Shakespeare's birth month. Heavy rain scrubbed the fireworks, and the river overflowed its banks even as *Soft Thou Gently Flowing Avon* was being sung. And most puzzling, almost nothing written by the Bard was performed. Samuel Foote found ample material for ridicule, satirizing this sort of retrospective in his 1768 play *The Devil Upon Two Sticks*: "A jubilee, as it hath lately appeared, is . . . an ode without poetry, music without melody, dinners without victuals, and lodgings without beds; a masquerade where half the people appear barefaced, a horse-race up to the knees in water."

japeworthy

Ridiculous; from *jape*, a trick, a jest.

—Thomas Tyrwhitt's *Glossary of the Poetical Works of Chaucer*, 1871

Oil of birch, a flogging with a birch rod. . . . Ignorant boys are frequently sent on the 1st of April for these refreshing stimulants.

—William Carr's *Dialect of Craven*, 1828

All Fools' Day

Archibald Armstrong became a renowned jester of England's James I, who allowed the entertainer's tongue full license. Armstrong was once the victim of a jest when he came to the house of a noble to bid him a prosperous New Year and was rewarded with several gold coins. Wishing to increase his gratuity, he grumbled and jingled them discontentedly, at which his patron requested their return. Archee complied, expecting more, but the noble simply put them in his pocket, remarking, "I gave my money into the hands of a fool, who had not the wit to keep it." Archee fell out of favor at court for calling Laud, the Archbishop of Canterbury, "a rogue and a traitor," and was physically kicked out of court with his coat pulled over his head — but not before he had amassed a considerable fortune, mainly from bribes for delivering petitions to the king. Archee retired and died in his native Arthuret, Cumberland, and was buried, appropriately enough, on All Fools' Day in 1672.

snickersneeze

A term without meaning used to frighten children. "I'll *snickersneeze* you."

—R. E. G. Cole's *Words Used in Southwest Lincolnshire*, 1886

Alpine Europe's Krampus Tradition

In some communities of Bavaria, South Tyrol, and Austria, such as the picturesque town of Salzburg, Austria, the hideous Krampus has long been believed to represent the dark side of St. Nicholas. Traditionally the Krampus has been depicted with reddened, deep-set, and malicious eyes, large goat-horns, a furry or leathery body, a long pointed tongue and teeth, cloven hooves and a tail, carrying rusty chains and birch switches with which to swat evil-doers. Occasionally, a picture will show him in a smart black or striped jacket, perhaps driving a car or even flying an airplane.

Beginning about December 5, this mythical monster has been thought to accompany St. Nick, who is obliged to hand over particularly incorrigible children and some adults to the Krampus for his Christmas dinner. Known variously as Knecht, Perchten, Pelznickel, Schmutzli, and Black Peter, a number of these places allow a "Krampuslauf" to take place in which drunken, costumed, torch-bearing revel-devils run through the streets, scaring children and adults alike. Of late, the Krampus has begun to appear in Christmas festivities in France and Finland, and even in San Francisco, Philadelphia and Portland, Oregon.

figaries

Showy or fantastic adornments.

—G. F. Northall's *Warwickshire Word-Book*, 1896

London's Lord Mayor's Show

was originally held on October 29 during most of its 900-year history. But in 1751, with Britain's calendar change, the date was moved to November 9, and then in 1959 to November's second Saturday. Beginning in 1422, displays were waterborne on the Thames, contributing to the parade term "float."

Peter Ditchfield's *Old English Customs* (1896) offered more on these events: "The Lord Mayor's Show is a familiar sight to Londoners, the sole survivor of the old pageants which delighted our forefathers when England's heart was young. The Lord Mayor still rides in his chariot of state, and a few of the companies send pageants — cars elaborately decorated and made to represent the particular craft with which the company is associated. Masses of fruit and flowers adorn the Fruiterers' Company. A band of neatly-dressed maidens show the skill of the Framework Knitters. But these are only relics of the grand spectacles that once graced the streets of the City. . . . Resplendent with gowns and hoods of diverse hues, the civic dignitaries, attended by the companies, used to march in procession through the streets to attend the services at St. Paul's Cathedral, and then entertained in their festal halls nobles and princes."

phantomnation

Appearance as a phantom.

— Sir James Murray's *New English Dictionary Supplement, Spurious Words*, 1933

Phantomatic, unreal. *Phantomic*, resembling a phantom.

— Sir James Murray's *New English Dictionary*, 1909

Grannows, streaks of dirt left in clothes from bad washing; the term is chiefly applied to body-linen.

— Georgina Jackson's *Shropshire Word-Book*, 1879

Washing the Sark

On Hallowe'en, a Border maiden may wash her sark and hang it over a chair to dry, taking care to tell no one what she is about. If she lie awake long enough, she will see the form of her future spouse enter the room and turn the sark. We are told of one young girl who, after fulfilling this rite, looked out of bed and saw a coffin behind the sark; it remained visible for some time and then disappeared". The girl rose up in agony and told her family what had occurred, and the next morning she heard of her lover's death. In another instance, the young woman is said to have seen her lover at first, but this image quickly vanished and was replaced by a coffin; she was shortly afterwards married to the man, but he soon died and left her a widow. I have heard of precisely the same practice in Ireland and in the county of Sussex.

— William Henderson's *Notes on the Folk-lore of the Northern Counties of England and the Borders*, 1866

ophicleide

A musical wind instrument of powerful tone, a development of the ancient "serpent," consisting of a conical brass tube bent double, with keys, usually eleven in number, forming the bass or alto to the key-bugle. . . . The euphonium is becoming the chief representative of the eight-foot octave among the brass instruments. *Ophicleidist*, a performer on the ophicleide.

—Sir George Grove's *Dictionary of Music*, 1902

Mardi Gras in New Orleans

It was about ten minutes past nine when the Carnival began to boom in the form of a most tremendous clamour of brass bands: shawm and pipe, psaltry, and *ophicleides* [see above] blown louder than ever, cymbal and triangles, and especially that very old friend of mine, the Big Drummer [depicted below]. He came along in the light of torches, drubbing away at the parchment as though for dear life. Last night he wore a splendid military uniform, and had on his shoulders epaulettes of red worsted as bright and big as prize tomatoes. But I was aware of him many years ago, when he wore a leopard-skin mantle and a brazen Roman helmet with a white plume. I was aware of him when he was in the service of a traveling dentist, when he administered a thundering whack to the drum simultaneously with the extraction by his patron of a patient's tooth. The whack drowned the patient's yell of agony.

—George Augustus Sala's *America Revisited*, 1883

bull's-noon

Midnight; a bull frequently breaking forth at that hour in search of adventures, as though it were midday instead of midnight. Suffolk & Norfolk.

—William Holloway's *Dictionary of Provincialisms*, 1838

The Minstrels' Festival of Tutbury

was held in mid-August for four centuries until the Duke of Devonshire abolished the proceedings in 1778. Until then, a "King of the Minstrels" and his four stewards were elected to preside over festivities and consider charges brought against unruly minstrels. The outgoing stewards ceremoniously furnished cakes, wine and ale to the accompaniment of spirited music, before the incoming officers provided the day's finale.

According to Robert Chambers's *Book of Days* (1864): "The conclusion of the day was much in accordance with the barbarous taste of the times. A bull being given them by the priory of Tutbury, they all adjourned to the abbey gate where . . . the minstrels rushed after the maddened creature, and if any could succeed in cutting off a piece of his skin before he crossed the river Dove into Derbyshire, he became the property of the King of Music. . . . But in the end the young men of the neighbourhood who flocked in great numbers to the festival could not help interfering with the minstrels . . . and this led to such outrage that many returned home with broken heads."

hangwit

A fine for the unjust hanging or escaping of a prisoner.

—Elisha Coles's *An English Dictionary*, 1713

Bastille Day

In 1789, disenfranchised Parisians helped touch off the French Revolution by storming and capturing the city's famous Bastille. But instead of the place which had over many decades come to symbolize royal abuse, the surprised liberators found very comfortable accommodations here, and just seven prisoners were incarcerated. Four of the inmates were counterfeiters, two were criminally insane, and one, the Count de Solanges, was moved there at his family's request because of the pleasant accommodations. After the Bastille was razed, the first six were re-arrested and locked up elsewhere, and only the Count remained at large.

According to a 2010 Parisian exhibit, the Bastille detained prostitutes, homosexuals and political dissidents, many of whom were affluent or well-off, rather than dangerous or common criminals. This luxury lock-up featured well-stocked fireplaces, very palatable wines and food, including pastries and first-rate health care was administered by the king's own doctor.

Detainees such as the acid-tongued philosopher Voltaire (shown here) entertained guests, and were even allowed to hold dinner parties. Despite being Paris's most heavily fortified building at that time, the Bastille was carefully destroyed by revolutionaries, and almost nothing of it remains.

agnominate

To nickname.

—Thomas Blount's *Glossographia*, 1656

Day of Public Humiliation

This gloomy March 10 "holiday" was instituted in the mid-1600s by Oliver Cromwell (shown here) and his Puritan followers, who subjected themselves to the bearing of such Bible-inspired names as Praise-God Barebones, among other things. Charles Bombaugh's *Gleanings for the Curious from Literature* (1874) listed these hyphenated Puritan names, followed by traditional surnames, drawn from a 1658 Sussex jury-list: "The-gift-of-God Stringer, Repentant Hazel, Be-thankful Playnard, Live-in-peace Hillary, The-work-of-God Farmer, Joy-from-above Brown, Be-of-good-comfort Small, Faint-not Hewett, Redeemed Compton, God-reward Smart, Kill-sin Pimple, Stand-fast-on-high Stringer, Seek-wisdom Wood, Fight-the-good-fight-of-faith White, Search-the-Scriptures Moreton, [and] Weep-not Billing." Bombaugh also mentioned a "Puritan maiden" who, when asked for hers, replied, "Through-much-tribulation-we-enter-the-Kingdom-of-Heaven — but for short they call me *Tribby*."

As late as the 1800s, these curious first names were used in Britain: Abishag, Amorous, Babberly, Brained, Bugless, Despair, Feather, Ham, Lettuce, Minniehaha, Murder, Uz, Water and Wonderful.

Maying

To go very early in the morning of the first of May into the fields or woods and gather green boughs to decorate people's houses. East Sussex.

—William Holloway's *Dictionary of Provincialisms*, 1838

Milkmaids on May Day

In his *Memoirs and Observations in his Travels Over England* (1719) Frenchman Henri Misson wrote: "On the 1st of May, and the five and six days following, all the pretty young country girls that serve the town with milk, dress themselves up very neatly and borrow abundance of silver plate, whereof they make a pyramid, which they adorn with ribbands and flowers, and carry upon their heads instead of their common milk-pails. In this equipage, accompany'd by some of their fellow milkmaids and a bagpipe or fiddle, they go from door to door, dancing before the houses of their customers, in the midst of boys and girls that follow them in troops, and everybody gives them something."

Eight decades later, Joseph Strutt noted in *Sports and Pastimes of the People of England* (1801): "The Mayings are in some [degree] yet kept up by the milkmaids at London, who go about the streets with their garlands, music, and dancing, but this tracing is a very imperfect shadow of the original sports; for May-poles were set up in streets, with various martial shows, morris-dancing, and other devices, with which revelling and good cheer the day was passed away. At night they rejoiced, and lighted up their bonfires."

Trades and Occupations

Oh, let us love our occupations,
Bless the squire and his relations,
Live upon our daily rations,
And always know our proper stations.

—Charles Dickens's novel, *The Chimes*, 1844

greenboarded

To be *greenboarded* is when a servant is [ushered] into the drawing-room, or elsewhere, before the master or mistress, to account for any misdoings.

—C. Clough Robinson's *Dialect of Leeds*, 1862

Porter's lodge, the usual place of summary punishment for the servants and dependents of the great, while they claimed and exercised the privilege of inflicting corporal chastisement.

—Robert Nares's *Glossary of the Works of English Authors*, 1859

Occupational Reset

Through the 19th century, a special hiring fair was held in Henley-in-Arden, Warwickshire and other English towns for servants who had either been involuntarily discharged or had second thoughts about working for their their employers. Ebenezer Brewer's *Dictionary of Phrase and Fable* (1898) explained: "In many places, 'statute fairs' are held where servants seek to be hired. Carters fasten to their hats a piece of whipcord; shepherds a lock of wool; grooms a piece of sponge, etc. When hired, they mount a cockade [badge of ribbon] with streamers. Some days after the statute fair, a second, called a *mop*, is held for the benefit of those not already hired. This fair *mops*, or wipes up, the refuse of the statute fair, carrying away the dregs of the servants left."

finedraw

To sew up a rent [rip] with so much nicety that it is not perceived. *Finedrawer*, one whose business is to sew up rents.

—Richard Coxe's *Pronouncing Dictionary*, 1813

Discerpible, that which may be torn asunder.

—John Boag's *Imperial Lexicon of the English Language*, c. 1850

Tailors Take It in the Shorts

Tailors were formerly known as the "ninth part of a man" — an attitude that Queen Elizabeth I seems to have condoned. John Farmer's *Slang and Its Analogues* (1890–1904) reported that she once addressed a "deputation of eighteen tailors" with the emasculating but mathematically correct salute, "God save you — gentlemen both." Seamsters were also disparaged with the proverb, "Nine tailors make a man." But according to A. Wallace's *Popular Sayings Dissected* (1895) this expression was a corruption of "nine *tellers* make a man," a *teller* being a church bell tolled nine times at a man's funeral — six being rung for a woman, and three for a child, but none for suicides.

C. H. Herford's *Notes on the Works of Shakespeare* (1902) commented on the expletive "tailor!" used in *A Mid-Summer Night's Dream*, which he deemed "an exclamation made in suddenly falling backwards, which [Samuel] Johnson remembered as being customary in his youth. Probably it was a mild execration connected with the traditional repute of tailors as thieves or cowards." Well into the 20th century, "son-of-a-tailor" was an insult.

back and edge

Completely, entirely; the back and edge being nearly the whole of some instruments.

—Robert Nares's *Glossary of the Works of English Authors*, 1859

Maintaining One's Edge

The anonymous cosmetic guide *Personal Beauty: The Whole Art of Attaining Bodily Vigor, Physical Development, Beauty of Feature and Symmetry of Form* (c. 1880) explained this curious and overlooked aspect of barbers' lore: "A single pair of razors is not sufficient for the beard of a man. . . . When a razor has been used for some time, it will lose its keenness without evident cause. But if left unused during a month or two, its fine edge will return without any fresh setting or sharpening. No reason for this has yet been assigned, though the fact is known to every barber. Three or four pairs of razors should be kept in constant use, and each razor brought into constant service not oftener than once in seven, eight, or nine days." This author added, "Grinding should never be resorted to."

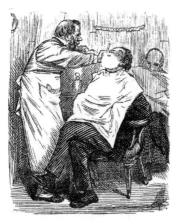

Alfred Ayres's *The Mentor* (1884) offered this explanation: "The microscope has shown that this tiring is due to the disarranging of the particles of steel, and that when a razor is allowed to rest for a sufficient length of time the particles readjust themselves, restoring the razor to its original usefulness."

cat-Latin

Incoherent or idle talk; bad writing.

—B. Kirkby's *Lakeland Words Used in Cumberland
and Westmoreland*, 1898

Wanted: A Perfect Typesetter

According to Henry Edwards's *Old English Customs: Curious
Bequests and Charities* (1842) a highly conditional annuity was
extended to London's Worshipful Company of Stationers by one
William Bowyer in his will, dated 30th July, 1777. Boyer understood
the needs of that organization and stipulated that their new hire
be a compositor "who shall usually frequent some place of public
worship every Sunday, unless prevented by sickness, and shall not
have worked on a newspaper or magazine for four years at least before
such nomination. He shall be able to read and construe Latin and
at least read Greek fluently, with accents, of which he shall bring
a testimonial from the rector of St. Martin's Ludgate for the time
being. I could wish that he shall have been brought up piously and
virtuously, if it be possible at Merchant Taylors' or some other public
school, from seven years of age till he is
full seventeen, and then to serve seven
years faithfully as a compositor
and work seven years more as a
journeyman, as I would not have
this annuity bestowed on anyone
under 31 years of age."

illaqueation

The act of ensnaring or trapping; from *illaqueate*, to ensnare.
—Rev. John Boag's *Imperial Lexicon of the English Language*, c. 1850

A snare; anything to catch another; a noose.
—Samuel Johnson's *Dictionary of the English Language*, 1755

The Life of a Ratcatcher

Ike Matthews's *Full Revelations of a Professional Rat-Catcher* (1898) offered readers a firsthand overview of his occupation (a rat-catcher is shown below) based on a quarter century of experience. In one passage he described traveling several hours by rail in Britain to and from his jobs, often transporting cages of rats, the ferrets who caught them and his dog: "I have often entered an empty third-class carriage, sent my dog under the seat, and put the rat-cage there also. The carriage would fill with passengers and upon reaching my destination I would take from under my seat my cage full of live rats, to the amusement of some and the disgust of others."

Once under contract, Ike would typically spend several months or more ridding buildings of vermin. He did not tolerate payment backsliders, remarking: "Should people decline to pay the bill [I had] the expedient of letting the rats at liberty again. Most people will pay the price rather than have the rats turned loose."

billingsgatry

Abusive language employed by those who are unable to come to an amicable understanding as to the proper price of the fish about which they are negotiating.

—Edward Lloyd's *Encyclopædic Dictionary*, 1895

Billingsgate dialect, scolding; ill language; foul words.

—B. E. Gent's *Dictionary of the Termes of the Canting Crew*, c. 1699

A Look Back at Billingsgate

In 1857, just before it was dismantled, Nathaniel Hawthorne visited and described in his *English Notebooks* London's venerable seafood bazaar known as Billingsgate: "We went along Lower Thames Street and quickly found ourselves in Billingsgate Market — a dirty, evil-smelling, crowded precinct, thronged with people carrying fish on their heads, lined with fish-stalls, and pervaded with a fishy odour.

The footwalk was narrow and filthy, and we had to elbow our way among rough men and slatternly women, and to guard our heads from the contact of fish trays. Very ugly, grimy, and misty, moreover, is Billingsgate Market, and though we heard none of the foul language of which it is supposed to be the fountainhead, yet it had its own peculiarity of behavior. For instance, Una tells me, one man staring at her and Miss Shepherd as they passed cried out, 'What beauties!' Another, looking under her veil, greeted her with, 'Good morning, my love!' Mamma and I were in advance, and heard nothing of these civilities, struggling through this fishy purgatory."

green labour

The lowest paid labour, especially in the tailoring trade. . . .
[From] German *ein grüner*, a green or foolish one; one who
is inexperienced, especially a recently arrived alien workman.
—Albert Hyamson's *Dictionary of English Phrases*, 1922

The Rise of the Luddites

Beginning late in 1811 in Nottinghamshire, and spreading quickly
throughout Yorkshire and Lancashire, a short-lived group of
reactionaries — who became known as Luddites, probably from a Ned
Ludd, who smashed some equipment in 1779 — began reacting to a
growing technological threat by going about sabotaging industrial
machinery. Some of the first targets were the looms of wool and
cotton mills, but later they included newfangled agricultural
mechanisms such as threshers, leading to the Swing Riots in southern
England in the 1830s.

Outside towns at night, many frightened workers met to plan
the destruction of automation tools, and then they
launched organized attacks. Their vandalism
was branded a capital offense by Parliament,
and dozens were executed or transported
to Australia for their violent opposition to
high-tech devices. Nowadays, the Luddites'
central principle — that it was wrong for
entrepreneurs to replace workers with
cheaper means of production — has, to some
degree, been superseded by the issue of jobs
being moved overseas.

acremen

Ploughmen; husbandmen.

—William Toone's *Etymological Dictionary of Obsolete and Uncommon Words*, 1832

Acreme, a law-word for ten acres of land.

—Edward Phillips's *New World of Words*, 1706

Plough Monday

On the first Monday after Christmas holidays, it was customary through the 19th century for English farm laborers, sometimes dressed in white and adorned with flowers and ribbons, to raise *plough-money* for drinking revelries. Joseph Taylor's *Antiquitates Curiosæ* (1819) mentioned, "The ploughmen in the North Country draw a plough from door to door, and beg money to drink. . . . It is conjectured that the system of begging money arose when they could not plough the land on account of its being frozen, as watermen drag about a boat in severe frosts and beg money because they are unable to ply on the river."

In *Those Superstitions* (1931), Charles Igglesden noted: "There was once among ploughmen a dislike to dig up an ancient coin in the fields. It meant the devil's curse, and the only antidote was to spit on each side of the coin. . . . It is interesting to recall that the ancient coins were at one time called 'hegs' in Kent, the word being derived from *hag*, or witch, and I was offered a 'heg penny' by an old ploughman . . . to keep away the Evil One."

headswoman

A midwife. It would be presumptuous to pry into obstetric mysteries to discover the origin or propriety of this denomination. We have no correspondent masculine noun. . . . Indeed, such a word as *headsman*, in this sense, must have been strangely ambiguous, for it signified also the executioner.

—Robert Forby's *Vocabulary of East Anglia*, 1830

Refined Execution

Charles-Henri Sanson (shown below) served the French Bourbon kings as an executioner for 38 years. Initially reluctant, he served Louis XVI, whom he beheaded in 1793, and the next year dispatched Maximilien Robespierre, a voice of reason during the French Revolution. While performing his duties, Sanson wore a blood-red coat and leggings, and in general brought a dignity to his office. Off duty, he played the violin and cello, and maintained relationships with such craftsmen as Tobias Schmidt, a respected German musical-instrument maker who built Sanson's guillotine. He also grew and compounded herbal remedies and dissected the bodies of some of his victims. At that time in French society, the executioner's position was hereditary, and as such these men, and occasionally women, married into one another's families.

After retirement, Sanson was introduced to Napoléon Bonaparte, who asked him how he could sleep well after executing nearly 3,000 people. Sanson retorted frankly, "If emperors, kings, and dictators can sleep well, why not an executioner?"

out of collar

Out of harness and the working habit. A horse has the collar slipped over its neck when put to work.

—Trench Johnson's *Phrases and Names: Their Origins and Meanings*, 1906

To die in harness, to die while employed, before retirement from work.

—Albert Hyamson's *Dictionary of English Phrases*, 1922

Work, Work, Work

In 1940, America's forty-hour workweek and a minimum wage of 25 cents per hour were begun as provisions of the Fair Labor Standards Act. A steady decrease in time spent on the job was recorded over the preceding century, and the rise of labor unions accelerated this trend, resulting in a 35% reduction of manufacturing work hours between 1900 and 1940, causing many economists and politicos to assume that this trend would continue. In 1933, Congress even considered the Thirty-Hour Work Week Bill, which was derailed by business interests after it was okayed by the Senate.

But expectations persisted. In 1956, for example, even conservative vice president Richard Nixon confidently predicted that Americans would work a four-day week in the "not so distant future." Three years later Edmund Ziegler agreed, writing in *The Nation*, "The extra day of leisure for Americans will have an effect as profound as that produced by the automobile."

colting

Romping in a very opprobrious sense, when applied to a woman.

—Frederick Elworthy's *Devonshire Glossary*, 1879

Colt, if applied to females, implies lewdness.... Hence *colting*, hoydenish, "loose."

—Joseph Wright's *English Dialect Dictionary*, 1898–1905

The Households of Henry VIII

An unpublished manuscript listed the following rules and prohibitions for one of Henry VIII's more than fifty households, many of which were considered palaces: "His Highness's attendants are not to steal any locks or keys, tables, forms, cupboards, or other furniture out of noblemen's or gentlemen's houses where they go to visit. Master cooks shall not employ scullions as go about naked or lie all night on the ground before the kitchen fire. No dogs shall be kept in the court, but only a few spaniels for the ladies.... The officers of his privy chamber shall be loving together; no grudging nor grumbling, nor talking of the king's pastime. There shall be no romping with the maids on the staircase, by which dishes and other things are often broken.... The pages shall not interrupt the kitchen-maids. Coal to be only allowed to the king's, queen's, and Lady Mary's chambers. The brewers are not to put any brimstone in the ale."

rats to all

All to pieces. Derbyshire.

—Samuel Pegge's *Supplement to the Provincial Glossary of Francis Grose*, 1814

The Pied Piper's Legend

or "Rat-catcher's Day," is still observed in Hamelin, Saxony, on June 26. With his famous flute, the legendary Pied Piper led 130 of the town's children away in 1284, never to be seen again. In the 16th century, the story was embellished to say that the piper's foul deed happened because he was not paid for ridding the town of rats. Whatever the truth was, English poet Robert Browning revived interest in this mystery with "The Pied Piper of Hamelin," a poem written about 1842 from a memory of his father's telling of it. One section reads:

> *Rats! They fought the dogs and killed the cats,*
> *And bit the babies in the cradles,*
> *And ate the cheeses out of the vats,*
> *And licked soup from the cooks' own ladles,*
> *Split open the kegs of salted sprats,*
> *And even spoiled the women's chats,*
> *By drowning their speaking*
> *With shrieking and squeaking*
> *In fifty different sharps and flats.*

blacksheep

To take another person's job; West Virginia; noted 1925.
—Harold Wentworth's *American Dialect Dictionary*, 1944

Britain's First Census

On about this date in 1801, Britain's first census was begun. In a subsequent survey conducted in 1881, residents were asked to furnish their "rank, profession, or occupation." Some of the more puzzling responses, as preserved by the London Genealogical Society, included:

- Colourist of artificial fish
- Knight of the Thimble
- Disinfector of railways
- Examiner of underclothing
- Invisible net maker
- Electric bath attendant
- Proprietor of midgets
- Fifty-two years an imbecile
- Knocker-up of workpeople

- Maker of sand views
- Gymnast to house painter
- Turnip shepherd
- Emasculator
- Sampler of drugs
- Fatuous pauper
- Drowner
- Count as female
- Fish-bender
- Goldfish-catcher
- Cow-banger
- Running about
- Grape-dryer
- Beef twister
- Random waller

friggle

To fidget, worry; to do anything in a slow or awkward way.

—Joseph Wright's *English Dialect Dictionary*, 1898–1905

Friggling, loitering or trifling about.

—J. Drummond Robertson's *Glossary of Archaic Gloucestershire Words*, 1890

A Close Shave

In the 1600s, barbershops were seen as places of idleness, and legislation was enacted to discourage loitering in such places. Some curious laws forbade customers from handling a barber's "surgical instruments" at a time when surgeries were undertaken there. These regulations were ridiculed as "laws for all faults" in Shakespeare's *Measure for Measure*, and homemade "rules" later satirized them. One such series of couplets, entitled "Rules for Seemly Behavior," was displayed in the 19th-century barbershops of Northallerton, Yorkshire:

Who checks the barber in his tale,
Must pay for each a pint of ale.
Who will or cannot miss his hat
While trimming, pays a pint for that.
And he who can or will not pay,
Shall be sent half-trimmed away.

The Natural World

This grand show is eternal. It is always sunrise somewhere; the dew is never all dried at once; a shower is forever falling; vapor is ever rising. Eternal sunrise, eternal sunset, eternal dawn and gloaming on sea and continents and islands, each in its turn, as the round earth rolls.

—*John of the Mountains: The Unpublished Journals of John Muir* (finally published in 1938)

dendranthropology

Study based on the theory that man had sprung from trees.
—T. Lewis Davies's *Supplementary English Glossary*, 1881

The Family Tree's Deep Roots

The writings of English antiquary and philosopher Sir Thomas Browne reflected a profound curiosity about the realm of nature, and served as an inspiration to many thinkers of his day. Although one of his major works, *Enquiries into Vulgar and Common Errors* (1646), focused on debunking everyday misconceptions — such as the idea that translucent rock crystals were merely "ice strongly congealed" — he himself was not immune from offering ludicrous explanations of natural phenomena.

His eccentric style and choice of topics made for unpredictable reading. Three centuries before the dawn of artificial insemination, with Britain dominated by Puritanism, Browne offered this dour commentary on human sexuality in *Religio Medici* (1643): "I could be content that we might procreate like trees, without conjunction, or that there were any way to perpetuate the world without this trivial and vulgar way of coition. It is the foolishest act that a wise man commits in all his life; nor is there any thing that will more deject his cooled imagination when he shall consider what an odd and unworthy piece of folly he hath committed."

clouder

An obsolete variant of *cludder*, a crowd, heap, cluster. *Clouder* is probably the same word as *clutter*, and is evidently the proper term for "a lot of cats."

—C. E. Hare's *The Language of Field Sports*, 1939

Cludder, *cluther*, a large quantity, or mass of anything gathered together.

—John Atkinson's *Glossary of the Cleveland* [Yorkshire] *Dialect*, 1868

Shrewdness of Apes

Mr. Hare's abovementioned book contained a litany of curious names formerly used for specific groups of animals. For example, among the smaller and more common British mammals he listed a *dray* of squirrels, a *bevy* of otters (used also for roe deer, quail, and larks), a *labour* of moles, a *richness* of martens, a *husk* of hares, a *glaring* of cats, a *dout* of feral cats, and a *business* of ferrets.

A century ago a group of monkeys was considered a *cartload*, several bears became a *sloth*, and herds of elk were known as *gangs*. Collections of lesser-known creatures were not overlooked. Companies of kangaroos and dogfish were also called *troops*, while on an African safari one's *sute* of bloodhounds or *cowardice* of curs might encounter a *sowse* of lions, a *leap* of leopards, or even a *shrewdness* of apes.

sheep's-eye

A modest, diffident or sly look, such as lovers cast at their mistresses.

—Richard Coxe's *Pronouncing Dictionary*, 1813

A wanton look.

—James Halliwell's *Dictionary of Archaic and Provincial Words*, 1855

To *cast a sheep's eye*, to look askance or sideways at one.

—Ebenezer Brewer's *Dictionary of Phrase and Fable*, 1898

The Proper Care of Sheep

Gervase Markham's *Cheap and Good Husbandry* (1613) offered shepherds some noteworthy techniques for restoring and maintaining relationships in their flocks: "If a lamb be born sick and weak, the shepherd shall fold it in his cloak, blow into the mouth of it, and then drawing the lamb's dug [utter] squirt milk into the mouth of it. If an ewe grow unnatural and will not take her lamb after she hath weaned it, you shall take a little of the clean of the ewe, which is the bed in which the lamb lay, and force the lamb to eat it, or at least chew it in her mouth, and she shall fall to love her lamb naturally. But if an ewe have cast her lamb, and you would have her take to another ewe's

 lamb, you shall take the lamb which is dead and with it rub and daub the live lamb all over, and so put it to the lamb, and she will take to it as naturally as if it were her own."

debacchation

A raging; a madness; from Latin *debacchatio.*

—Samuel Johnson's *Dictionary of the English Language*, 1755

[From] *debacchate*, to revile one after the manner of drunkards.

—Henry Cockeram's *Interpreter of Hard English Words*, 1623

Mad as a March Hare

The skittish reputation of the March hare quietly survived into Victorian times, when Lewis Carroll immortalized it in *Alice's Adventures in Wonderland*. Numerous references to this creature exist in English literature, including one from Shakespeare's *The Two Noble Kinsmen*, in which the bard refers to "a dainty madwoman . . . as mad as a March hare." This animal's notoriety was questioned as early as 1567 by John Heywood, who asked, "Are not midsummer hares as mad as March hares?"

The phrase was used as early as the 1400s, and John Skelton included the simile 'as mer[r]y as a Marche hare' in *Magnyfycence: A Goodly Interlude* (c. 1520). *March-mad* was defined in Rev. James Stormonth's *Dictionary of the English Language* (1884) as "rash to an extreme," in allusion to March being the rutting time of hares, "when they are very excitable." Stormonth also defined "mad as a March hare" as "mad as a hare in rutting season, when they are wild, flighty, and strange." The phrase "March madness" was not applied to American college basketball playoffs until 1991.

arborescent

Resembling a tree; partaking of the nature and habits of a tree.

— John Ridpath's *Home Reference Library*, 1898

Keeping Track of Nature

English naturalist Robert Marsham (1708–1797) conceived and developed the science of what was eventually named "phenology" in the 1840s. The October 1884 edition of the journal *Nature* referred to phenology as "the observation of the first flowering and fruiting of plants, the foliage and defoliation of trees, the arrival, nesting, and departure of birds, and such like, which has attracted the attention of naturalists from time to time for nearly 150 years." A quarter century later, the *New English Dictionary* defined phenology as "the study of the times of recurring natural phenomena in relation to climatic conditions."

Marsham's painstaking pioneering work began in earnest on his Norfolk country estate in the spring of 1736. There, he carefully noted details of the English seasons coming and going — an activity that would continue for the next six decades and serve as a basis for the current concern over climate change. Marsham (shown at left)

depicted here eventually gathered enough material to assemble his best-remembered writing, *Indications of Spring*, drawn from his meticulously kept records of the weather, bird migrations, and observations of many obscure natural events, which attracted the admiration of such noteworthy thinkers as Thomas Jefferson.

dejecture

Excrements; *dejectory*, tending to promote evacuations
by stool.

—B. E. Gent's *Dictionary of the Termes of the Canting Crew*, c. 1699

Excess of animal secretions, as of perspiration, sweat, liquid
dejectures, &c.

—John Arbuthnot's *Concerning the Nature of Ailments*, 1731

Call It What You Will

The indelicate subject of animal excreta was apparently discussed
with far more ease and precision in earlier times, as suggested by the
following group of archaic terms for the leavings of specific creatures.
John Kersey's *New English Dictionary* (1772) included *trettles* ("the
dung of a rabbet") and *lesses* ("the dung of a boar, bear, or wolf") while
B. E. Gent's *Dictionary of the Canting Crew* (1699) offered *billeting*
("foxes' excrement") as well as *spraints* or *spraintings*, which came
from otters. Elsewhere, James Halliwell's *Dictionary of Archaic
and Provincial Words* (1855) furthers our knowledge of this arcane
subject, contributing *ging*, "excrementum,"
along with the less ambiguous *fuants*, "dung
of the wolf, fox, marten, or badger ... *crotels*,
the ordure of hare, rabbit or goat, also
called *croteys* and *crotising*," adding
"*fewmets*, the dung of deer, also called
fewmishings" and "*werdrobe*, the ordure of
the badger." Halliwell concluded with the
oddity "waggying," the droppings of foxes.
Painting by Albrecht Dürer.

hippophageous

Horse-eating. From Greek *hippo*, a horse, and *phago*, to eat.
—Daniel Lyons's *American Dictionary of the English Language*, 1897

Morse, the hippopotamus; the river horse.
—John Ash's *Dictionary of the English Language*, 1795

Bon Appétit!

Francis Trevelan Buckland (1826–1880) was a British surgeon, second-generation naturalist and a pioneer of zoöphagy, or meat-eating. He founded Britain's Society for the Acclimatization of Animals, whose mission was to increase local food production by broadening what could be considered pleasantly edible. His father, William, who in 1824 became the first person to document a fossil, was also known for dishing up unusual fauna to guests, including crocodile, panther and bluebottle flies, and made a stuffed-animal menagerie of his home.

In 1859, Mr. Buckland found himself in charge of a large dinner party in which he offered such exotic entrees as kangaroo, ostrich, Southeast Asian sea slugs and even "mouse on toast." Over the next 20 years, he enjoyed serving other delicacies in his London home, like boiled elephant trunk, rhinoceros pie, slug soup, horse's tongue, squirrel pie, porpoise heads and stewed mole, and he offered many recipes to the public.

gussock

A strong and sudden gush of wind. Norfolk.

—William Holloway's *Dictionary of Provincialisms*, 1838

The Old Language of Windmills

European windmills, used most commonly in the Low Countries, have long been used to display a variety of events, including births, deaths, marriages, holidays such as Christmas and one's child passing exams. Charles Igglesden's *Those Superstitions* (1931) noted these specific messages once conveyed by windmills: "When the four arms were standing as a simple vertical cross, the mill was being repaired. . . . When a member of the family died, the mill was put into mourning, and the degree of mourning was governed by fixed rules of windmill etiquette. If the owner died, all the twenty boards in the arms were taken out and the mill stood motionless for a time. When church bells tolled marking the procession of the funeral to the grave, the boardless blades were turned in unison with the bells. When the wife of a miller died, nineteen boards were removed; for a child of the miller, thirteen; for the miller's parents, eleven; and so on down to the children of cousins, for whom one board was removed. For many generations the miller made his mill express his joys and sorrows [and it] could convey its message to everyone in sight."

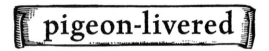

pigeon-livered

Mild in temper; soft; gentle.
—Rev. John Boag's *Imperial Lexicon of the English Language*, c. 1850

Farewell to the Passenger Pigeon

In 1914 the last passenger pigeon, which had once darkened the sky in eastern America and southern Canada, died in the Cincinnati Zoo. Three centuries earlier, when as many as ten billion of them were alive, French explorer Samuel Champlain marveled at their numbers, and about 1700, Cotton Mather estimated a migrating flock to be a mile wide, requiring several hours to pass. One 850-square-mile nesting area in Wisconsin was home to an estimated 136 million of these birds about the time that John Audubon journaled in 1813 that the sky was "black with birds" for three days.

These birds were decimated by encroaching settlements, by deforestation, and by hunters who plied them with alcohol-laced grain before shooting them to feed to pigs and slaves. Large sulfur

fires were even set to smoke nesting birds from trees. In 1896, sportsmen who knew that these birds were endangered, destroyed the last wild flock, numbering a quarter million. Too late, states such as Michigan, which harvested up to a billion one year, passed laws to protect them with enclosures. But these gregarious birds would only breed when large groups congregated, and rarely in captivity.

secretist

One who has special skill in any . . . special or private information.

—Sir James Murray's *New English Dictionary*, 1914

No Theory for Man or Beast

William Rutty (1687–1730), osteology lecturer and member of England's Royal Society, wrote to a colleague in 1828. He confided that his decades of work with anatomical specimens had led him to believe that a biological link intertwined members of the animal kingdom, including mankind: "While anatomising, I am often struck by the similarities between the bodily structures of animals with one another, and even with those corresponding in men. Yea, tails are found on many beasts, and their locomotion is accomplish'd on four legs, but I must, with God as my witness, admit that the similarities are far more common than are the differences." He concluded gingerly, "I trust that my thoughts will remain in your confidence, as I dread that some or many would find my suspicions — that beasts and men have common ancestry — to constitute an unbearable heresy."

His secret was dutifully maintained. Charles Darwin (shown here) would not publish his shocking treatise, *On the Origin of Species*, which proposed that mankind had evolved through natural selection, for another 131 years. This work was written without the benefit Rutty's insights.

fit for the fox farm

Old and broken down; usually of an animal. In reference to the feeding of horsemeat to foxes being raised for fur. Chiefly Wisconsin.

—Frederic Cassidy's *Dictionary of American Regional English*, 1991

At strawheft is said of horses who are stalled with too heavy a load and obliged to rest at intervals.

—Thomas Darlington's *The Folk-Speech of South Cheshire*, 1887

Hobson's Choice

In Britain and America we still occasionally hear people refer ironically to a limited option meaning. This proverbial expression was derived from a business practice of Thomas Hobson (1544–1631), who kept a 40-horse stable in Cambridge, where he stubbornly allowed customers to take only the mount beside the barn door. Many were young, impatient students traveling to London who often rode the horses too hard. Steele wrote of Hobson's system of rotation which allowed animals to recover: "When a man came for a horse, he was led into the stable [and] . . . he obliged him to take the horse which stood next to the stable door, so that every customer was alike well served. . . . From whence it became a proverb, when what ought to be your election was forced upon you, to say *Hobson's Choice*." Of Hobson's demise, John Milton wrote tenderly that death

Show'd him where he must lodge that night,
Pull'd off his boots and took away the light;
If any asked for him, it shall be said,
Hobson has supp'd and newly gone to bed.

napiform

Having the form, shape, or appearance of a turnip; from Latin *napus*, turnip.

—Sir James Murray's *New English Dictionary*, 1914

Runaway-crop, thin or bad crop of turnips. Isle of Wight.

—James Halliwell's *Dictionary of Archaisms and Provincialisms*, 1855

Britain's Turnip Tricentennial

Henry Graham's *The Social Life of Scotland in the Eighteenth Century* (1899) described the rise of the humble turnip, which turned out to be well suited for British farmers and their livestock: "Although introduced into England from Holland in 1716, turnips were only sown by two or three energetic proprietors before 1739, and being sown in little patches broadcast and never hoed, they naturally failed. Great excitement was caused about Melrose [Scotland] in 1747 by the rumour that a strange new vegetable was to be sown. When it sprang up, the curious people pulled up these odd weeds to examine them. When the bullocks were fed on the turnips they grew so big that people accustomed to stunted creatures would not eat such monsters. So late as 1774, farmers in Dumbartonshire would not sow them, although stimulated by bribes. Treated as delicacies, Captain Topham was amused to see turnips in Edinburgh used as part of the dessert at the principal houses."

Tales and Travails of Travel

Never any weary traveler complained that he came too soon to his journey's end.

—Thomas Fuller's *Good Thoughts in Bad Times*, 1863

simmiting

Fondness for a person of the opposite sex. *Simmity*, to look after admiringly.

—R. Pearse Chope's *The Dialect of Hartland, Devonshire*, 1891

Love in the Country

W. C. Hazlitt's *Faiths and Folklore of the British Isles* (1870) explained a curious custom in rural England and northern Europe called *bundling*: "Bundling used to be a widely diffused Welsh custom before marriage. The betrothed or engaged pair went to bed, or more frequently lay together, in their clothes [often with feet tied together]. Even among families of good position it is tacitly recognized and tolerated, and it was at the outset the product of the clothed state, where touch had to play the part of sight in the unclothed."

Francis Grose's *Classical Dictionary of the Vulgar Tongue* (1796) added that it was "practised in America [due to] a scarcity of beds where, on such an occasion, husbands and parents frequently permitted travelers to bundle with their wives and daughters."

Margaret Baker's *Folklore and Customs of Rural England* (1974) presented an accessory item: "Prudent mothers gave daughters approaching the bundling age a 'courting-stocking,' completely covering the girl's body from the waist downwards, with room for both legs within it. Such stockings ... were often heirlooms." Rev. Samuel Peters's *General History of Connecticut* (1781) added, "Bundling has prevailed 160 years in New England. ... Bundling takes place only in the cold seasons of the year."

258   *The Best of Forgotten English*

God's time

Formerly, time as told by the sun, as opposed to standard time. Later, standard time as opposed to Daylight Savings Time.

—Frederic Cassidy's *Dictionary of American Regional English*, 1991

Travel Time

In 1883, the use of tidy modern standardized time zones was introduced in Canada, but America waited another 35 years, until 1918, to formally follow suit. Before then, local municipalities were free to set their own times, usually based on solar calculations, and kept time on town hall clocks or even on timepieces in a jeweler's front window. As a result, neighboring towns had slightly differing times, making such activities as rail travel more confusing.

The English created standardized time zones as early as 1847. The Royal Observatory in Greenwich began telegraphing the time to British towns and cities a few years later in 1852, and this became the standard of time, even abroad. However, as this passage from John Sandilands's *Western Canadian Dictionary and Phrase-Book* (1913) showed time was far from standardized even then: "The difference between Canadian time and Greenwich or London time is as follows: "Halifax, Nova Scotia, 4 hours 14 minutes [earlier than London]; Montreal, 4 hours 54 minutes; Winnipeg, 6 hours 28 minutes; Vancouver, 8 hours 12 minutes. Thus, when it is midday in London, it is 8:46 a.m. in Halifax."

circumbendibus

A roundabout way.
—Bennett Wood Green's *Word-Book of Virginia Folk-Speech*, 1899

Strange Bedfellows

English army captain Frederick Marryat (1792–1848) visited America in the latter 1830s. In his *Diary in America*, published in 1839 after his return home, he described meager roadside accommodations which awaited weary travelers: "He who is of the 'silver-fork school' will not find much comfort out of the American cities and towns. There are no neat, quiet little inns, as in England. When you stop at humble inns you must expect to eat peas with a two-pronged fork and to sit down to meals with people whose exterior is anything but agreeable, and to sleep in a room in which there are three or four other beds — I have slept in one with nearly twenty — most of them carrying double. A New York friend of mine travelling with his family told me that in a Western inn he had particularly requested that he might not have a bed-fellow, and was promised that he should not. On retiring he found his bed already occupied, and went down to the landlady and expostulated. 'Well,' replied she, 'it's only your own driver; I thought you wouldn't mind *him*!'"

In 1874, the waterfront Grand Hotel was opened in Stockholm, Sweden, and a second owned and managed by the same company in Oslo, Norway — the first hotels to offer every guest the luxury of freshly-laundered bedsheets.

barrow-back't

Bent by heavy work such as wheeling loaded barrows.
—Alexander Gibson's *The Folk-Speech of Cumberland*, 1880

Krohn's Wheelbarrow Tour

In June, 1908 John Albert Krohn set off from Portland, Maine after loading his necessities into a homemade wooden wheelbarrow. He had long wanted to see America and was ready for a change from newspaper work. So, combining the two motives, he trudged off, hoping to sell his story when he returned. Keeping the interior of America on his left, he walked the 46-state perimeter, first heading across New Hampshire, Vermont, and upstate New York, then along the Great Lakes to northern Minnesota, where he skirted the Canadian border due west, all the way to Washington.

On his 13-month journey — which took him down the Pacific Coast to Southern California, eastward across several deserts to Louisiana and the Gulf of Mexico, and finally up the Atlantic seaboard to where he began — he wore out three tires, 121 pairs of socks, and 11 pairs of shoes. Along his 9,024-mile sojourn, he was welcomed heartily and received many overnight accommodations, meals and places for repair and recuperation, as well as many goodwill cards to decorate his vehicle. He saw his story published about 1910 as *The Walk of Colonial Jack: A Story of a Long-Distance Walker*.

bittock

A distance of undecided length. If a North countryman be asked the distance to a place, he will most probably reply, "a mile and a *bittock*." The latter may be considered any distance from one hundred yards to ten miles.

—John Camden Hotten's *Slang Dictionary*, 1887

Of time; from *bit*, and *ock*, a diminutive suffix. "Edinburgh University is three hundred years old — or rather, three hundred years and a *bittock*."

—John Farmer's *Slang and Its Analogues*, 1890–1904

If you ask a Scotchman the distance to any place, he will reply, after asking you in return where you came from, that it is so many miles and a *bittock*.

—James Maitland's *American Slang Dictionary*, 1891

The Waywiser

In 1657, English diarist John Evelyn wrote: "I went to Colonel Blount, who showed me the application of the *way-wiser* to a coach, exactly measuring the miles and showing them by an index as we went on. It had three circles, one pointing to the number of rods, another to the miles, by 10 to 1000, with all subdivisions of quarters; very pretty and useful." In 1701, Joseph Moxon's *Mathematical Instruments* mentioned a personal "waywiser for the pocket" containing "a movement, like a watch, to number or count your steps or paces in order to find how far you walk."

farlies

Strange things, wonders. *Ferlies* (or *fairlies*) is in common use in Scotland for "sights, show things to be seen." . . . [From] Middle English *ferly*, strange, wonderful; Old English *færlic*, sudden, unexpected.

—Walter Skeat's *Glossary of Tudor and Stuart Words*, 1914

Wonderclout, something showy but worthless.

—Sir James Murray's *New English Dictionary*, 1928

To Go or Not to Go?

Besides being a remarkable lexicographer, as well as a critic and a poet, Samuel Johnson (1709–1784) was a reasonably good traveler, as represented by his friend and biographer James Boswell in *The Life of Samuel Johnson* (1791). In December 1779, Dr. Johnson commented on one of Ireland's most amazing natural wonders, the remote coastal outcropping of cuboid rocks in county Antrim known as Giant's Causeway. When asked how interesting this place might be to a tourist, he made this distinction: "Worth seeing? Yes, but not worth *going to see*." An example of Johnson's subtle but profound influence on future generations of writers may be noticed in such modern guidebooks as the prestigious Michelin series, begun by Édouard Michelin about a century after Johnson's statement. The guides have long embraced Johnson's concept on the subject, rating destinations with such terminology as "interesting" and "worth a detour," as well as those they classify as "worth a journey."

passager

A traveller or voyager.

—Rev. John Boag's *Imperial Lexicon of the English Language*, c. 1850

The Travels of Sir Richard Burton

(1821–1890) arguably Britain's greatest explorer, as well as a geographer, poet, writer, diplomat, and spy. Burton (shown here) suffered incurable wanderlust that would lead him across Europe, Asia, and India, where he served in the East India Company, as well as North and South America. His insatiable appetite for new horizons took him into the heart of Africa, where he sought the source of the Nile and became the first European to view Lake Tanganyika. He mastered twenty-nine languages, introduced English speakers to the *Kama Sutra* in 1883 and an updated version of *The Arabian Nights* two years later, and wrote many articles and books inspired by his extensive expeditions.

In 1853, he traveled in Pashtun disguise to Mecca, once forbidden to non-Muslims. His ruse worked, but one night he was discovered, after lifting his robe to urinate instead of squatting, as an Arab would do. He managed to talk himself out of this predicament, which might have cost him his life, and lived to publish his account of Mecca

through the eyes of a Western imposter.

In 1863, Burton cofounded the Anthropological Society of London, whose mission was, in Burton's words, "to supply travellers with an organ that would rescue their observations from the outer darkness of [unpublished] manuscript and print their curious information on social and sexual matters."

miscasualty

Mischance, mishap.

> —Sir James Murray's *New English Dictionary*, 1908

An unlucky accident. And why is it not as good a word as *mischance* or *misfortune*?

> —Rev. Robert Forby's *Vocabulary of East Anglia*, 1830

An Early Traffic Accident

A *Diary in America* (1839), compiled by English visitor Frederick Marryat, included this observation of coach travel: "I was upset [overturned] twice in one half hour when I was travelling in the winter time, but the snow was very deep at the time, and no one thinks anything of an upset in America. More serious accidents do, however, happen. When I was in New Hampshire, a neglected bridge broke down and precipitated coach, horses, and passengers into a torrent which flowed into the Connecticut River. Some of the passengers were drowned.

"Those who were saved sued the township and recovered damages, but these *mischances* [see above] are to be expected in a new country. The great annoyance of these public conveyances is that neither the proprietor nor driver consider themselves servants of the public. A stagecoach is a speculation by which as much money is to be made as possible."

son of the morning

A traveller, in allusion to the practice in the East of travellers rising early in order to avoid the fatigue of travelling in the heat of the day. *Traveller's license*, exaggeration, in allusion to the reputation acquired by travellers.

—Albert Hyamson's *Dictionary of English Phrases*, 1922

A Search for Welsh Indians

John Evans (1770-1799) an idealistic Methodist from Caernarvonshire, Wales, set out to find the descendants of a long-lost tribe of Welsh-speaking Indians in April 1795. In Wales, Evans had heard a ridiculous tale of this particular tribe, whose members were supposed to be Welshmen who had discovered America in 1170. Known as the Mandans, they were rumored to be living near the headwaters of the Missouri River. Driven by an urge to rescue and convert these "countrymen" and improve their miserable lives, Evans secured funding for his expedition from the Welsh Methodist Church. Anticipating the Lewis and Clark expedition by eight years, Evans set out in April 1795, but returned home the next year after an 1,800-mile sojourn. His journey resulted in the charting of a stretch of the Missouri, which was of some help to Lewis and Clark.

Later, he wrote to a friend in Philadelphia, "I am able to inform you that there are no such people as the Welsh Indians." Dejected, he died in New Orleans a few years afterward, perhaps from alcohol consumption.

ruttier

An old traveler acquainted with roads; an old soldier; from *route*, French *router*.

—Noah Webster's *American Dictionary of the English Language*, 1828

Come Fly with Me

In 1930, Ellen Church went on duty aboard a Boeing Air Transport flight between Oakland and Chicago, becoming the airline industry's first "stewardess" at a time when male "stewards" handled mail, issued tickets, and served snacks. Right up into the 1950s, a flight attendant was required to have a medical background, often including a nurse's certification, due to the many hazards, including an outright crash, which could befall passengers.

Arthur Frommer's 1957 classic, *Europe on 5 Dollars a Day*, described a money-saving plan offered routinely by trans-Atlantic airlines: "Buy a round-trip ticket to the most distant city on your itinerary. Under the 'multi-stopover plan' (some airlines call it the 'extra-city system') you can stop as long as you wish in any of the major cities along the route. A round-trip ticket to Rome, for instance, permits no less than seventeen stops. On the way to Rome, you can stay at Glasgow, Belfast, Manchester, London, Amsterdam, Brussels, Paris, Zurich, Geneva, and Nice. On the return trip you can stop, again for as long as you wish, at Milan, Stuttgart, Munich, Frankfurt, Hanover, and Bremen. . . . This extra mileage comes to you free under the multi-stopover plan."

raccoons and alligators

It has been pouring [raining] what we in England vulgarly term "cats and dogs," but which on the politer shores of the Mississippi might be called "raccoons and alligators."
—George Sala's *America Revisited*, 1883

Jonas Hanway

was an English import merchant whose travels took him to many distant realms, including Asia. He received an abundance of ridicule for being the first to carry an umbrella in the streets of London as protection — not from sun, but from rain. When his contrivance began to catch on, London hackney coachmen felt particularly threatened by Hanway's adaptation of the parasol for wet weather, as walkers became less dependent on their services.

Robert Chambers's *Book of Days* (1864) reported that in the early 1750s, "a gentleman did exercise the moral courage to use an

umbrella in the streets of London. . . . A *parapluie* defended Mr. Hanway's face and wig. For a time, no others than the dainty Macaronies ventured to carry an umbrella. Anyone doing so was sure to be hailed by the mob as 'a mincing Frenchman.' Once John Macdonald found as late as 1770 that, on appearing with a fine silk umbrella, he was saluted with the cry of 'Frenchman, why don't you get a coach?'"

whenny-megs

Trinkets.

—J. Drummond Robertson's *Glossary of Archaic Gloucestershire Words*, 1890

East Meets West

Historian William Robertson (1721–1793) described Columbus's first moments in the New World: "The inhabitants appeared in the simple innocence of nature, entirely naked. Their black hair, long and uncurled, floated upon their shoulders, or was bound in tresses around their heads. They had no beards, and every part of their bodies was perfectly smooth. Their complexion was of a dusky copper colour, their features singular rather than disagreeable, their aspect gentle and timid. Though not tall, they were well shaped and active. Their faces and several parts of their body were fantastically painted with glaring colours. They were shy at first through fear, but soon became familiar with the Spaniards, and with transports of joy received from them bawksbells, glass beads, or other baubles, in return for which they gave such provisions as they had, and some cotton yarn, the only commodity of value that they could produce. . . . The former, enlightened and ambitious, formed already vast ideas with respect to the advantages which they might derive from the regions that began to open to their view. The latter, simple and undiscerning, had no foresight of the calamities and desolation which were approaching their country."

fogo

A disagreeable smell.

—Jabez Good's *Glossary of East Lincolnshire*, 1900

Graveolent, having a strong or unpleasant smell.

—Rev. John Boag's *Imperial Lexicon of the English Language*, c. 1850

No Pleasure Cruise

On this date in 1840, French diplomat Adolphe Fourier de Bacourt left Bristol, England, for America. In his memoirs, published as *Souvenirs of a Diplomat* (1885), he described his ship's steerage section: "The engine and 'menagerie' occupy the centre [near] the cabins of the domestics, those of the crew, and the kitchens. . . . God help the nervous invalids who live there. In this space are packed together eighty-five passengers — men, women, and children — and ninety-two of the crew . . . justly celebrated for their disagreeable odor. Then there are two cows, twelve pigs, ten sheep, twenty-five chickens, and as many ducks, geese, and turkeys. . . . Imagine all these drinking, eating, sleeping, crying, singing, bellowing, bleating, and add to this the noise of the engine and the orders for the management of the vessel. Imagine yourself shut up in a stateroom seven feet long, seven feet wide, and seven feet high, and you will have a correct idea of the pleasure of the voyage. . . . If the sea is rough half of these people are sick, and so are the animals; then it becomes an infernal abode."

spoom

To be driven swiftly.

—Rev. John Boag's *Imperial Lexicon of the English Language*, c. 1850

Roading, running races with teams upon the road.

—William Marshall's *Provincialisms of East Norfolk*, 1787

Around the World in 24 Weeks

A 13,340-mile automobile race was won by a 60-horsepower, American-built Thomas Flyer, driven by Yankee George Schuster and two assistants (shown here) in 1908. Starting at a raucous Times Square in New York on February 12 the six contestants — three French, one Italian, one German, and Schuster — drove their unique vehicles (one outfitted with mast and sail!) up the Hudson River to Albany, then eastward through Chicago to San Francisco. From there, the cars were shipped to Yokohama, where they roared across Japan before being ferried to Vladivostok, Russia.

Wearing goggles and fur coats, the two drivers and one mechanic per vehicle were often forced to improvise routes, since roads and maps were scarce in many places. In Siberia, the Germans and Americans jockeyed for the lead, with the others far behind. All three French vehicles eventually dropped out, leaving the Americans, Germans and Italians to win, place and show, respectively. The Americans crossed the Paris finish line 11 days before the Germans and two weeks before the Italians.

Bygone Religious Practices

The easy confidence with which I know another man's religion is folly teaches me to suspect that my own is also.

—Mark Twain, as found in Albert Paine's *A Biography: The Personal and Literary Life of Samuel Langhorne Clemens*, 1912

bag of nails

A state of confusion or topsy-turveyism. From *bacchanals*. Thieves' cant.

—John Farmer's *Americanisms, Old and New*, 1889

Hubbleshew, a riotous assembly. Northern England.

—Francis Grose's *Provincial Glossary*, 1811

The Casting of the Stools

A small church riot broke out at St. Giles's Church in Edinburgh in 1637 after King James I attempted to impose a series of Roman Catholic reforms on the Church of Scotland. Robert Chambers's *Book of Days* (1864) reported: "There were no pews in those days; each godly dame sat on her own chair, or clasp-stool, brought to church on purpose. When the dean . . . opened the service book and began to read the prayers, this multitude was struck with a horror which defied all control. They raised their voices in . . . abusive language, denouncing the dean as the progeny of the devil, and the bishop as a belly-god, calling out that it was rank popery they were bringing in. A strenuous female threw her stool at the dean's head, and whole sackfuls of small clasp-bibles followed. After the formal dismissal of the congregation, the bishop was mobbed on the street, and narrowly escaped with his life. . . . The Civil War, which ended in the destruction of the royal government twelve years after, might be said to have begun with the Casting of the Stools."

tarans

The little spectres, or souls of unbaptised infants [who] were often seen flitting among the woods and secret places, bewailing in soft voices their hard fate.

—Thomas Pennant's *A Tour in Scotland*, 1769

Buzzalogue, an exchange of gossip.

—Maurice Weseen's *Dictionary of American Slang*, 1934

Sources of Gossip

Georgina Jackson's *Shropshire Word-Book* (1879) offered background regarding an earlier meaning of *gossip*: "*Gossip* is still used by our peasantry in its first and etymological sense, namely as a sponsor in baptism — one sib, or akin in God, according to the medieval Church, that sponsors contracted a spiritual affinity with one another, with the parents, and with the child itself."

Richard Trench's *Select Glossary of English Words Used Formerly in Senses Different from Their Present [Ones]* (1859) continued this explanation: "*Gossips*, in this primary sense, would ordinarily be intimate and familiar with one another or would have become so; and thus the word was next applied to all familiars and intimates. At a later day it obtained the meaning which is now predominate in it, namely the idle, profitless talk, the *commérage* (which word has exactly the same history) that too often finds place in the intercourse of such [people]."

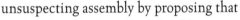

farrups

A word used in expressions of surprise, chiefly by older people. "What the *farrups* are ye at?"

—Alfred Easther's *Glossary of Almondbury and Huddersfield*, 1883

Ferrups, an exclamation of mild imprecation, especially in the phrase, "by the *ferrups!*" Yorkshire, Lancashire, Cheshire, and Derwentwater.

—Joseph Wright's *English Dialect Dictionary*, 1898–1905

Sa-ant my Bob, interjection of surprise. Probably an intentional deformation of "So help me God."

—Thomas Darlington's *The Folk-Speech of South Cheshire*, 1887

An Odd Tribute to Edward the Confessor

In 1885, the feast of England's Edward the Confessor, a group of latter-day Catholic "pilgrims" gathered at the Anglo-Saxon king-saint's monument at Westminster Abbey, which Edward founded in the 11th century. At this event, Catholic Cardinal Manning shocked the unsuspecting assembly by proposing that  the Church of England should return to the "fold" of the Roman Catholic Church, from which it was separated by Henry VIII in 1534. The annual visits to the abbey continued on this date, but the puzzling reunification proposal, after once raising eyebrows among Catholics and Anglicans alike, failed to arouse much interest and was never brought up again.

dog-rapper

A church beadle or sexton. Dogs having ceased to be a common nuisance as intruders into church, *dog-rapping* has passed into oblivion. But the practice survived for a time for the discipline of children in church.

—Edward Gepp's *Essex Dialect Dictionary*, 1923

The office was anciently a paid one and known as that of the "dog-whipper."

—John Wilkinson's *Leeds Dialect Glossary and Lore*, 1924

Order in the Church

In old times, many individuals considered it their duty to set aside part of their worldly wealth for keeping the congregation awake. On the 17th April, 1725, John Rudge bequeathed to the parish of Trysull, in Staffordshire, twenty shillings a year that a poor man might be employed to go about the church during sermon and keep the people awake; also to keep dogs out of church. Some curious provisions were made for this purpose. A bequest by Richard Dovey, of Farmcote, dated in 1659, had in view the payment of eight shillings annually to a poor man for the performance of the same duties in the church of Claverley, Shropshire. . . . At Dunchurch a similar custom existed. A person bearing a stout wand, shaped like a hayfork at the end, stepped stealthily up and down the nave and aisle and, whenever he saw an individual asleep, he touched him so effectively that the spell was broken, this being sometimes done by fitting the fork to the nape of the neck.

—Robert Chambers's *Book of Days*, 1864

libidinosity

Lustfulness, lasciviousness, luxury, incontinency.
—Thomas Blount's *Glossographia*, 1656

Libidinist, a lustful person; a lecher; formed on Latin *libido*, lust.
—Sir James Murray's *New English Dictionary*, 1908

Ruttish, wanton; libidinous; lecherous.
—John Walker's *Dictionary of the English Language*, 1835

Concupiscent, libidinous; lecherous.
—William Grimshaw's *Ladies' Lexicon and Parlour Companion*, 1854

Hanky Panky in Church

In 1667 London diarist Samuel Pepys candidly noted his risky and unorthodox behavior at a religious service: "Being wearied, I turned into St. Dunstan's Church, where I heard an able sermon and stood by a pretty, modest maid, whom I did labour to take by the hand and the body; but she would not, but got further and further from me, and at last I could perceive her to take pins out of her pocket to prick me if I should touch her again, which seeing I did forbear, and was glad I did spy her design. And then I fell to gaze upon another pretty maid in a pew close to me, and she on me; and I did go about to take her by the hand, which she suffered and withdrew. So the sermon ended and the church broke up, and my amours ended also; and so took a coach home, and there took up my wife."

assishness

Blockishnesse [stupidity].
—John Florio's *Queen Anna's New World of Words*, 1611

Moke, slang name for a donkey or ass. The word was first used in this connection in 1848. [Forty years earlier,] *moxio* was the gipsy name for a donkey.
—Edwin Radford's *Unusual Words and How They Came About*, 1946

The Feast of the Ass

anciently celebrated at Beauvais, France annually on the 14th of January, commemorated the flight of the Virgin into Egypt with the infant Jesus. To represent the Virgin, the most beautiful girl in the city, with a pretty child in her arms, was placed on an ass richly caparisoned. Thus mounted, she preceded the Bishop and his clergy, and they all went in grand procession from the cathedral to the church of St. Stephen. On entering the chancel, they [ar]ranged themselves on the right side of the altar. . . . Parts of the service were terminated by [an] imitation of the braying of an ass . . . and hymns were sung in praise of the ass.
—William Hone's *Ancient Mysteries Described*, 1823

Followed by the bishop and clergy, she . . . celebrated mass, not forgetting to explain the fine qualities of the animal, and exhorting him to make a devout genuflection, with a variety of other fooleries.
—Rev. Charles Buck's *A Theological Dictionary*, 1835

biblioclast

A destroyer of books, or the Bible.

—Sir James *Murray's New English Dictionary*, 1888

Biblical Bloopers

In 1517, the Church forbade the printing of any book — particularly the Bible — without permission. Since then, printings of the Bible have contained curious errors, among them a 1632 edition called the *Wicked Bible* which omitted *not* in the Seventh Commandment, leaving "Thou *shalt* commit adultery." A 1652 Cambridge Press undertaking, dubbed the *Unrighteous Bible*, posed the rhetorical question in 1 Corinthians 6:9, "Know ye not that the *unrighteous* shall inherit the Kingdom of God?" The 1551 *Bug Bible* was so named after an erroneous translation of *bogies* to *bugges* in Psalm 91:5, yielding, "Thou shalt not be afraid of *bugges* by nighte." As late as 1833, Noah Webster published a "sanitized" Bible, replacing such libertine terms as "give suck" with "nourish." In Isaiah 24:9, the "Beer Bible" was created by the replacement of "strong drink" with "beer."

Perhaps the most noteworthy variant was one printed in 1579, which became known as the *Breeches Bible* because in Genesis 3:7 *breeches* was substituted for *aprons* in describing how Adam and Eve "sewed figge-tree leaves together and made themselves breeches." This passage contributed to the use of fig-leaf concealment in Western Art.

daffle

To betray loss of memory and mental faculty. Persons growing old and in their dotage are said to *daffle* and be *daffers*.

—John Brockett's *Glossary of North Country Words*, 1825

Rev. William Spooner

(1844–1930) was a London-born scholar who lectured on divinity, philosophy, and ancient history at Oxford's New College. A contemporary described him physically as "an albino, small, with a pink face, poor eyesight, and a head too large for his body."

Although loved and respected by those who knew him, he sometimes displayed outward signs of being a proverbial absent-minded professor. His frequent verbal miscues gave the name *Spoonerism* to a form of spoken faux pas in which portions of words are humorously transposed — a trait Spooner downplayed. For example, students during a chapel service once heard the master of transposition utter "these beery wenches" when referring to the pews — instead of "these weary benches." In another instance, Spooner toasted Queen Victoria, exclaiming, "Three cheers for our *queer old dean*." Dozens of his other goofs were recorded, including "It is *kisstomary* to *cuss* the bride," along with "the lord is a *shoving leopard*," and "*well-boiled icicle*" for *well-oiled bicycle*. He even poured wine onto spilled salt, and remarked of a widow that "her husband was eaten by missionaries" in Africa.

genethliacks

The science of calculating nativities, or predicting the
future events of life from the stars predominant at birth.

—Samuel Johnson's *Dictionary of the English Language*, 1755

Second Coming — Take Two

On October 22, 1844, a recalculated "second coming" failed to
materialize for the followers of "Father" William Miller (1782–1849).
In New England, farmers who had steadfastly refused to plant their
fields that spring as a sign of their faith were deeply saddened by this
nonevent, and some were reported to have "wept till dawn." Seventeen
months earlier, on June 7, 1843, thousands of Miller's disciples,
who lived between the farmlands of Illinois and the towns of New
England, had donned white muslin gowns in preparation for the end
of the world.

According to John Farmer's *Americanisms, Old and New* (1889),
"Numbers of his followers settled their earthly accounts, bade farewell

to their friends, put on their 'ascension
robes,' and listened for the sounding
of the last trumpet. The highways and
byways were thronged with anxious
crowds of men and women, while the
trees in the orchards and the roofs of
houses were filled with more impatient
Millerites who thus hoped to be nearer to
their new home in Heaven."

half-named

A child privately baptized, but not christened in church.
—G. C. Lewis's *Provincial Words Used in Herefordshire*, 1839

Perilous Winter Baptisms

Sir John Sinclair's *Statistical Account of Scotland* (1794) cautioned new parents about cold-weather christenings: "There is one pernicious practice that prevails much in this parish, [Kilfinan, Argyleshire, Scotland] that of carrying their children out to baptism on the first or second day after birth. Many of them, although they had it in their option to have their children baptised in their own houses by waiting one day, prefer carrying them seven or eight miles to church in the worst weather in December or January, by which folly they too often sacrifice the lives of their infants to the phantom of superstition."

But two centuries earlier, Reginald Scot's *The Discovery of Witchcraft* (1584) warned readers not to delay: "The devil teacheth witches to make ointments of . . . children, whereby they ride in the air and accomplish all their desires. So, if there be any children unbaptized, or not guarded with the sign of the cross, then witches may and do catch them from their mothers' sides at night."

Sidney Addy's *Household Tales with Other Traditional Remains* (1895) added, "Children who are ill-tempered before baptism will be good-natured after they have been baptized. They will also sleep better and thrive."

beating the bounds

On Ascension Day, it used to be customary for the parish school children, accompanied by the clergymen and parish officers, to walk through their parish from end to end. The boys were struck with willow wands all along the lines of the boundary before maps were common. The boys were thus taught to know the bounds of their parish.

—Ebenezer Brewer's *Dictionary of Phrase and Fable*, 1898

Open-Air Revelry

Frederick Hackwood's *Inns, Ales and Drinking Customs of Old England* (1909) gave this holy day name new meaning while describing an elevating tradition — devised to impress local geographic boundaries on youngsters — that was practiced on Ascension Day: "Everyone who has read of these perambulations knows how largely the drinking of ale entered into their observance, and this under the eye and tacit consent of the Church. The clergy and choristers always headed the procession, which not only included

the principal parishioners, but tailed off into the boys and youths, and all the riffraff of the neighbourhood, the main attraction being the bountiful supplies of ale which were freely distributed at certain inns and stopping-places along the line of the parish boundaries. The drinking at the inns was not considered an unfit concomitant with the reading of the gospel at various 'gospel trees' along the route."

torvous

Sour of aspect; stern; severe of countenance.

—Samuel Johnson's *Dictionary of the English Language*, 1755

Puritans Suppress the Theater

In 1642 the English Parliament, dominated by the Puritans, drafted the following ordinance, which effectively closed down theaters across Britain: "Whereas, the distracted state of England, threatened with a cloud of blood by a civil war, call for all possible means to appease and avert the wrath of God. . . . It is therefore thought fit, and ordered by the Lords and Commons in this Parliament assembled, that while these sad causes and set times of humiliation do continue, public stage-plays shall cease and be forborne." Under this and subsequent statutes, actors and other theater employees were arrested, jailed and severely punished, which could involve a public flogging, banishment or a trip to the gallows if they were unwilling to renounce their stage livelihoods. Even members of the audience were fined five shillings if caught at a performance. But royalty and aristocrats circumvented this legislation until the Restoration reopened the theaters eighteen years later.

Looking back, H. L. Mencken, the "Bard of Baltimore," described Puritanism in his *Chrestomathy* (1949) as "The haunting fear that someone, somewhere, may be happy."

jack-o'-the-clock

In old clocks, a figure which struck the bell to mark the hours.

—John Phin's *Shakespeare Cyclopædia and Glossary*, 1902

Minute-jack, the figure that strikes the bell of a clock.

—William Toone's *Etymological Dictionary of Obsolete and Uncommon Words*, 1832

For Whom the Bell Tolls

Not everyone has appreciated the quaint sound of bells, even on Sundays, as we read in George Sala's *America Revisited* (1883): "The bell-ringing nuisance is nearly as offensive in England as it is in America, and in both countries the practice is equally needless and wantonly indifferent to the requirements of those who need rest and quiet. Surely a man knows to what religion he belongs and at what hour the services in his particular place of worship begin. Yet the sexton goes on tugging at his bell as though Christians had altogether lost their memories, and as though there were no clocks and watches in the world. Moreover, how is the churchgoer to discriminate between the different bells when they are all brangling at the same time? Here in Baltimore, a city of 300,000 inhabitants, there are about 200 churches.

With the exception of the Quakers' meeting-houses, all these churches are provided with bells which boom and brawl from sunrise to sunset, as though they were so many hotel gongs calling guests to theological meals."

bondieusard

Dealer in articles used for worship in churches.

—Albert Barrère's *Argot and Slang Dictionary*, 1911

Brooklyn, City of Churches

Evacuation Day marks the anniversary of the date in 1783 when British troops occupying Brooklyn finally went home, and was once observed as a public holiday. English wordsmith John Farmer, in his *Americanisms, Old and New* (1889), bluntly described this date as "the end of a mad king's folly."

Shortly afterward, during the early 19th century, Brooklyn became known as the "City of Churches" because of its numerous places of worship. But by mid-century, with its church construction not keeping pace with other cities', it was clear that on a per-capita basis the city would soon outgrow its nickname. By 1880, Cincinnati's 204 churches — one for every 1,253 residents, compared to a 1:1,988 ratio in Brooklyn — had overshadowed Brooklyn's, but it never claimed the quaint "City of Churches" moniker. In fact, Philadelphia, with its 593 churches, also eclipsed Brooklyn, with twice its total number and a 1:1,427 ratio. New York City also boasted 200 more churches than her smaller neighbor. But somehow, as the demographics changed, Brooklyn retained its old reputation for churches.

Forgotten Phrases
and Vocabulary

It is much to be wished that the publication of the county
dialects of England should go on. It will restore to us our
language in all shades of variation. It will incorporate into
the present one all the riches of our ancient dialects, and
what a store this will be may be seen by running the eye over
the county glossaries and observing the words we have lost
by abandonment and disuse, which in sound and sense are
inferior to nothing we have retained. . . . A language cannot
be too rich.

—Thomas Jefferson, in a letter to Englishman
John Evelyn Denison, 1825

A

abracadabrant
Marvellous; from *abracadabra*, a magic word used in the Middle Ages.
—Albert Barrère's *Argot and Slang Dictionary*, 1911

algates
Used to express different meanings, as *always, nevertheless, by all means*.
—William Toone's *Etymological Dictionary of Obsolete and Uncommon Words*, 1832

amatorculist
A little insignificant lover; a pretender to affection.
—Samuel Johnson's *Dictionary of the English Language*, 1755

audit ale
Extra strong ale, supposed to be drunk when the accounts are audited.
—John Camden Hotten's *Slang Dictionary*, 1887

B

baby-farm
A place where young children are received to nurse for payment.
—Edward Lloyd's *Encyclopædic Dictionary*, 1895

bedsister
Concubine.
—Herbert Coleridge's *Dictionary of the First, or Oldest Words in the English Language*, 1863

bedswerver
An adulteress, one who *swerves* from the fidelity of the marriage bed.
—Robert Nares's *Glossary of the Works of English Authors*, 1859

beggars' velvet
Downey particles which accumulate under furniture from the negligence of maids.
—John Camden Hotten's *Slang Dictionary*, 1887

blatteration
Senseless roar; from Latin *blatteratio*. *Blatent*, bellowing, as a calf.
—Samuel Johnson's *Dictionary of the English Language*, 1755

blissom
Of sheep, to desire the male; from Old Norse blœr, a ram.
—Hensleigh Wedgwood's *Dictionary of English Etymology*, 1878

boutisale
A sale by a lighted match, during the burning of which a man may bid.
—Rev. John Boag's *Imperial Lexicon of the English Language*, c. 1850

boy scout's leave
Shore leave requiring early return on shipboard. *Royal Australian* Navy slang.
—Sydney Baker's *Popular Dictionary of Australian Slang*, 1943

bubulcitate
To make a cry like a cow-herd.
—Thomas Blount's *Glossographia*, 1656

buzznacking
Gossiping from place to place.
—Francis Robinson's *Words Used in the Neighbourhood of Whitby*, 1876

C

cacozealous
Ill-affected or badly imitating. Viciously devout.
> —Edward Phillips's *New World of Words*, 1696

calebasses
Large, soft breasts; literally, gourds.
> —Albert Barrère's *Argot and Slang Dictionary*, 1911

calzoons
Drawers; breeches.
> —C. A. M. Fennell's *Stanford Dictionary of Anglicised Words and Phrases*, 1964

chantepleure
One that sings and weeps at the same moment. Of French *chanter*, to sing, and *pleurer*, to weep. Chaucer.
> —Nathaniel Bailey's *Etymological English Dictionary*, 1749

chiliagon
A plane figure of a thousand angles and sides; [from] Greek *chilia*, a thousand, and *gonia*, an angle.
> —Rev. John Boag's *Imperial Lexicon of the English Language*, c. 1850

chollers
Lumps of fat beneath the chin; double chins.
> —John Mactaggart's *Scottish Gallovidian Encyclopedia*, 1824

circumforaneous
Wandering from house to house, as a *circumforaneous* fiddler.
> —William Toone's *Etymological Dictionary of Obsolete and Uncommon Words*, 1832

clawscrunts
Old trees which cattle rub themselves against.
> —John Mactaggart's *Scottish Gallovidian Encyclopedia*, 1824

comb the head
Instead of combing the hair, they always *comb the head*.
> —Bennett Green's *Word-Book of Virginia Folk-Speech*, 1899

copulatives
Persons intending to marry. *Twelfth Night*.
> —C. H. Herford's *Notes on the Works of Shakespeare*, 1902

cow-tongued
Having a tongue smooth one way and rough the other, like a cow. Applied to one who gives fair or foul language as may suit his purpose.
> —James Halliwell's *Dictionary of Archaic and Provincial Words*, 1855

cupidity
An eager desire to possess something; an ardent wishing or longing; an inordinate or unlawful desire of wealth or power.
> —Rev. John Boag's *Imperial Lexicon of the English Language*, c. 1850

D

dingclicker
An unusually fine or pleasing person or thing. Maine.
> —Harold Wentworth's *American Dialect Dictionary*, 1944

diseases of the south
The south wind was thought to be charged with noxious influences.
—C. H. Herford's *Notes on the Works of Shakespeare*, 1902

doomsman
Judge.
—Herbert Coleridge's *Dictionary of the First, or Oldest Words in the English Language*, 1863

dormiat
A license to sleep. The licensed person is excused from attending early prayers in the chapel, from a plea of being indisposed. From Latin, *let him sleep.*
—Benjamin Hall's *Collection of College Words and Customs*, 1856

double-eyed
Having a deceitful countenance. *Double-hearted*, having a false heart; deceitful; treacherous. *Double-tongued*, making contrary declarations on the same subject at different times.
—Rev. John Boag's *Imperial Lexicon of the English Language*, c. 1850

dry smoke
When without tobacco, an inveterate smoker will sometimes pull at an empty pipe. This is known as a *dry smoke.*
—Charles Pettman's *Africanderisms: South African Colloquial Words*, 1913

dwiming away
Gradually wasting from disease. From Anglo-Saxon *dwínan.*
—Edward Sutton's *North Lincolnshire Words*, 1881

E

eftsoones
Again, often.
—John Bullokar's *English Expositor*, 1616

Englifier
One who renders a work into English; a translator.
—Sir James Murray's *New English Dictionary*, 1901

enterlean
With alternate layers of lean and fat meat; usually applied to bacon, which is always classified as "fat and interlean."
—R. Pearse Chope's *The Dialect of Hartland, Devonshire*, 1891

ept
Appropriate; effective; used as a deliberate antonym of *inept.*
—Sir James Murray's *New English Dictionary*, 1897

exflunct
To demolish. Also *exfluncticate* and *exflunctify.*
—Richard Thornton's *American Glossary*, 1912

eyebite
To fascinate or bewitch by a certain influence from the eye.
—Edward Phillips's *New World of English Words*, 1658

eyeservant
One who works only while watched, or while his master is present.
—James Barclay's *Dictionary of the English Language*, 1848

F

false generations
Bastard offspring. *Cymbeline.*
—C. H. Herford's *Notes on the Works of Shakespeare*, 1902

fantoosh
Flashy; ultra-fashionable.
—Mairi Robinson's *Concise Scots Dictionary*, 1985

farding-bag
The first stomach of a cow or other ruminating animal.
—Cuthbert Johnson's *Farmer's Encyclopædia of Rural Affairs*, 1844

flitflats
"Give one the *flitflats*," make one nervous. Central Kansas, 1914.
—Harold Wentworth's *American Dialect Dictionary*, 1944

flobbage
Phlem.
—Sir James Murray's *New English Dictionary*, 1901

floption
All of a *floption*, unawares; Newfoundland, c. 1895.
—Harold Wentworth's *American Dialect Dictionary*, 1944

fourth-class liberty
Scanning the shore with binoculars, when restricted aboard ship.
—Gershom Bradford's *Glossary of Sea Terms*, 1943

Frenchman
Any man, of any country, who cannot speak English.
—Walter Rye's *Glossary of Words Used in East Anglia*, 1895

frummagemmed
Annhilated, strangled, garroted, or spoilt. Old cant.
—Albert Barrère's *Dictionary of Slang, Jargon and Cant*, 1897

full of
In frequent use in various parts of South Africa in the sense of *covered with.*
"The child is *full of* mud" means the child is covered with mud.
—Charles Pettman's *Africanderisms: South African Colloquial Words*, 1913

G

galactic
Pertaining to milk; galactic acid, the acid of milk. *Galactologist*, one who
subsists on milk; from Greek *gala*, and *phago*, to eat.
—Rev. John Boag's *Imperial Lexicon of the English Language*, c. 1850

galligaskins
Wide hose or breeches, so called because worn by the Gascoigns.
—Thomas Blount's *Law Dictionary and Glossary*, 1717

gay Quaker
A quaker dressing less soberly than others.
—Richard Thornton's *American Glossary*, 1912

geloscopy
A sort of divination performed by means of laughter; or a divining any person's qualities or character by observation of the manner of his laughing.
—Nathaniel Bailey's *Etymological English Dictionary*, 1749

gemmosity
The quality of being a jewel.
—Samuel Johnson's *Dictionary of the English Language*, 1755

glonders
In the glonders, in a state of ill humour, to be pouting.
—John Jamieson's *Etymological Dictionary of the Scottish Language*, 1808

gone to the bottom
When a Nantucketer drops a thing, he is apt to speak of it as having *gone to the bottom*.
—William F. Macy's *Nantucket Scrap Basket*, 1930

groundstalworth
Strongly and firmly fixed in the ground, like a tree or a well-built edifice.
—Charles Mackay's *Lost Beauties of the English Language*, 1874

H

handsignment
A signature. Eastern Canada.
—Harold Wentworth's *American Dialect Dictionary*, 1944

hanging day
In America, Friday.
—Richard Thornton's *American Glossary*, 1912

healsfang
The sum every man sentenced to the pillory would have had to pay to save him from that punishment.
—Benjamin Thorpe's *Ancient Laws and Institutes of England*, 1840

heart-quakes
Tremblings of the heart.
—Robert Nares's *Glossary of the Works of English Authors*, 1859

henchboy
A kind of page; an attendant.
—Joseph Worcester's *Dictionary of the English Language*, 1881

hen's-nosefull
A very small quantity of anything.
—James Halliwell's *Dictionary of Archaic and Provincial Words*, 1855

history of the four kings
A pack of cards.
—George Matsell's *Vocabulum, or The Rogue's Lexicon*, 1859

honeyfuggle
To deceive, hoodwink, cheat a person; to obtain by duplicity.
—Mitford Mathews's *Dictionary of Americanisms*, 1956

horse-furniture
The trappings of a horse, including saddle, bridle, etc.
—William Whitney's *Century Dictionary*, 1889

husbandically
Economically.

—Sir James Murray's *New English Dictionary*, 1901

I

iatromathematique
A physician and mathematician that cures in a mathematical way.

—Elisha Coles's *An English Dictionary*, 1713

illiac passion
A painful wringing or twisting of the guts.

—John Kersey's *New English Dictionary*, 1772

in ponticalibus
In pontifical ornaments. Said of a bishop clad in his proper vestments, or of any person wearing his best apparel.

—John Kersey's *New English Dictionary*, 1772

isabelline
This colour is a whitish yellow, or buff colour, a little soiled. The archduke Albertus, who had married the infant Isabella, daughter of Philip II, King of Spain [laid] siege to Ostend. His pious princess, who attended him in that expedition, made a vow that till it was taken she would never change her clothes. Contrary to expectation, as the story says, it was three years before the place was reduced, in which time her highness's linen had acquired the abovementioned hue.

—Joseph Taylor's *Antiquitates Curiosae*, 1819

J

Jerusalem-pony
A donkey, evidently allusive to our Savior's entrance into Jerusalem on an ass.

—G. F. Northall's *Warwickshire Word-Book*, 1896

Jinking's hen
A hen that never knew the cock; metaphorically used for an old maid.

—John Mactaggart's *Scottish Gallovidian Encyclopedia*, 1824

jockum-gage
A chamber-pot. "Tip me the *jockum-gage*," hand me the member-mug.

—Capt. Alexander Smith's [Glossary from] *A Complete History of the Lives and Robberies of the Most Notorious Highwaymen, Footpads, Shoplifts & Cheats of Both Sexes*, 1719

joliflitch
Pleasantly.

—Herbert Coleridge's *Dictionary of the First, or Oldest Words in the English Language*, 1863

Judas-colour
Red. A red beard was called a *Judas-coloured* beard. Essex.

—James Halliwell's *Dictionary of Archaic and Provincial Words*, 1855

K

kabobbed
Dressed savory as a kabob.

—Robert Hunter's *Encyclopædic Dictionary*, 1894

key of the street
An imaginary ailment, said to be possessed by anyone locked out of doors.
—John Camden Hotten's *Slang Dictionary,* 1887

kingling
A little king.
—John Boag's *Imperial Lexicon of the English Language,* c. 1850

kurfuffling
The disarrangement of a person's clothes, hair, in rough play.
—Michael Traynor's *The English Dialect of Donegal,* 1953

L

lightning-before-death
Exhilaration which is supposed to occur in some instances just before death.
—C. T. Onions's *Oxford Shakespeare Glossary,* 1911

liripipionated
Hooded; wearing the *liripoop.*
—T. Lewis Davies's *Supplementary English Glossary,* 1881

lollicker
The tongue.
—Jabez Good's *Glossary of East Lincolnshire,* 1900

long hundred
One hundred and twenty. *Long dozen,* thirteen.
—Albert Hyamson's *Dictionary of English Phrases,* 1922

lum o' a day
A very wet day. The rain is *lumming* down when it rains fast. This word and *loom,* a mist or fog, are kindred.
—John Mactaggart's *Scottish Gallovidian Encyclopedia,* 1824

lutherhood
Wickedness; from *luther,* wicked. Also *lutherness.*
—Herbert Coleridge's *Dictionary of the First, or Oldest Words in the English Language,* 1863

M

mallemarocking
The visiting and carousing of seamen in the Greenland ships.
—Admiral William Smyth's *Sailor's Word-Book,* 1867

mammiformis
Shaped like a breast or teat.
—Tarton's *Medical Glossary [of Termes] Deduced from their Original Languages,* 1802

manurable
That which may be cultivated. [Related to] *manurage,* cultivation.
—John Boag's *Imperial Lexicon of the English Language,* c. 1850

Master of the Rolls
A baker. *Master of the Mint,* a gardener.
—Albert Hyamson's *Dictionary of English Phrases,* 1922

matrimonial polka
Copulation.
—John Farmer's *Slang and Its Analogues,* 1890–1904

matriotism
Love of one's mother country; from *patriotism.*
—Sir James Murray's *New English Dictionary*, 1908

meacock
An uxorious, effeminate man. Lame; cowardly; from *meek* and *cock.*
—John Boag's *Imperial Lexicon of the English Language*, c. 1850

milkscore
Account of milk owed for, scored on a board.
—Richard Coxe's *Pronouncing Dictionary*, 1813

mistress-piece
Capital distinction, as applied to a woman. [Similar to *masterpiece.*]
—John Boag's *Imperial Lexicon of the English Language*, c. 1850

mulligrubs
Ill temper; sulkiness; as to "have the *mulligrubs.*"
—Bennett Wood Green's *Virginia Folk-Speech*, 1912

N

Narrowdale noon
To put off doing something until Narrowdale noon is to defer it forever.
Narrowdale is a local name for the narrowest part of Dovedale, Derbyshire. The
few cotters who dwell there never see the sun throughout the winter, and when
its beams pierce the deep dale in the spring it is only for a few minutes in the
late afternoon.
—Edwin Radford's *Encyclopædia of Phrases and Origins*, 1945

neezled
A little drunk or intoxicated.
—Walter Skeat's *North of England Words*, 1873

ninety-nines
In the phrase, "done up to the *ninety-nines,*" well-groomed and dressed.
—Michael Traynor's *The English Dialect of Donegal*, 1953

nixnuts
Applied to a person who is neither clever nor capable. It is used also of a rogue.
From German *nichtnutz,* useless, worthless.
—Charles Pettman's *Africanderisms: South African Colloquial Words*, 1913

nocent
Guilty; criminal; the opposite of *innocent.* From Latin *nocens.*
—William Toone's *A Glossary and Etymological Dictionary of
Obsolete and Uncommon Words* 1832

O

odds and evens
To be at *odds and evens,* to differ in opinion. Westmoreland.
—Albert Hyamson's *Dictionary of English Phrases*, 1922

oof
A slang term for money derived from the legendary "oof bird." From Latin
ovum, an egg, which traces its origin to the goose with the golden eggs.
—Trench Johnson's *Phrases and Names: Their Origins and Meanings*, 1906

ooth
Raging mad; from German *wuth*, and Scottish *wud*.
—Charles Mackay's *Lost Beauties of the English Language*, 1874

opusculum
A little work; an opuscule.
—C. A. M. Fennell's *Stanford Dictionary of Anglicised Words*, 1964

P

pay in cats and dogs
To pay, not in cash, but in inconvenient or useless commodities.
—Richard Thornton's *American Glossary*, 1912

periblepsis
A delirious stare of the eyes.
—John Redman Coxe's *Philadelphia Medical Dictionary*, 1817

pigsnye
A diminutive of pig; a burlesque term of endearment.
—Robert Nares's *Glossary of the Works of English Authors*, 1859

poor-man-of-mutton
The remains of a shoulder of mutton broiled for supper.
—Alexander Warrack's *Scots Dialect Dictionary*, 1911

porculation
A feeding of swine.
—Henry Cockeram's *Interpreter of Hard English Words*, 1623

prairie-bitters
A beverage compounded of buffalo gall and water in the proportion of a gill to a pint. It is a mixture the medicinal virtue in an exact ratio to its filthy taste.
—John Farmer's *Americanisms, Old and New*, 1889

puckersnatch
A difficulty; a complicated situation. Southern Vermont.
—Vermont Historical Society, 1959

pugnuckling
Fornicating. Invented by Faulkner for his novel, *The Reivers* (1962).
—Calvin Brown's *Glossary of Faulkner's South*, 1976

pulpatoons
Delicacies; from Latin *pulpamentum*.
—William Toone's *A Glossary and Etymological Dictionary of Obsolete and Uncommon Words*, 1832

pupule
Crazy; insane. A crazy person.
—John Reinecke's *Loanwords from the Hawaiian Language*, 1938

Q

quafftide
Time of drinking.
—T. Lewis Davies's *Supplementary English Glossary*, 1881

quickscented
Having an acute perception by the nose; [related to] *quicksighted.*
—Rev. John Boag's *Imperial Lexicon of the English Language*, c. 1850

quincunx
A plantation of trees, disposed originally in [London's] squares consisting of five trees, one at each corner and a fifth in the middle.
—William Grimshaw's *Ladies' Lexicon and Parlour Companion*, 1854

quirboilly
Boiled leather; from Old French *cuir*, leather.
—Alois Brandl's *Glossary of Middle English Literature*, 1949

quisquilious
Of the nature of rubbish or refuse.
—Sir James Murray's *New English Dictionary*, 1909

quotationipotent
Powerful in quotation.
—T. Lewis Davies's *Supplementary English Glossary*, 1881

R

ramjollock
To shuffle cards.
—John Farmer's *Slang and Its Analogues*, 1890–1904

razorable
Fit to be shaved.
—John Walker's *Dictionary of the English Language*, 1835

red-lattice phrases
Talk appropriate to taverns of the lowest class, denoted by red lattice.
—C. H. Herford's *Notes on the Works of Shakespeare*, 1902

rempuceller
To apparently restore virginity.
—John Farmer's *French-English Dictionary of Erotica*, 1896

rewish
Vehement in copulation.
—John Minsheu's *Guide into Tongues*, 1617

rib wrenches
A slang name for spurs.
—Ramon Adams's *Western Words: A Dictionary of the Range, Cow Camps, and Trail*, 1946

riparian
Belonging to a river bank; from Latin *ripa*, a river bank.
—Daniel Lyons's *American Dictionary of the English Language*, 1897

rocking chair money
Unemployment compensation. Pacific Northwest.
—Walter McCulloch's *Woods Words: A Comprehensive Dictionary of Logger's Terms*, 1958

running banquet
In the original sense, a hasty refreshment.
—John Phin's *Shakespeare Cyclopædia and Glossary*, 1902

runnion
The male organ; Chaucer.
—Sir James Murray's *New English Dictionary*, 1914

S

sacking-law
The craft of the brothel-keeper.
—A. V. Judges's *The Elizabethan Underworld Glossary*, 1930

saggitary
A centaur — half man, half horse — armed with a bow. Shakespeare.
—Thomas Browne's *Union Dictionary*, 1810

scallibrat
A noisy, screaming child; loud and vituperative language.
—Rev. Marmaduke Morris's *Yorkshire Folk-Talk*, 1892

Scotch coffee
Burned biscuit in hot water.
—Frank Bowen's *Sea Slang: The Old-Timers' Expressions*, 1929

sexangularly
Hexagonal; having six corners or angles.
—Thomas Browne's *Union Dictionary*, 1810

sharooshed
Taken aback; surprised; disappointed; disgusted. Newfoundland.
—Harold Wentworth's *American Dialect Dictionary*, 1944

shoespoon
A shoehorn.
—Henry Shoemaker's *Old Time Words Used in Pennsylvania*, 1930

side-cousin
An illegitimate relative.
—T. Lewis Davies's *Supplementary English Glossary*, 1881

skookum house
A jail; a place of detention. Pacific Northwest.
—William Craigie's *Dictionary of American English*, 1940

slept in age
Advanced in years; from Old English *stæppan*, to proceed.
—Walter Skeat's *Glossary of Tudor and Stuart Words*, 1914

slut-hole
A hiding-place for dirt. A household word.
—John Ogilvie's *Comprehensive English Dictionary*, 1865

slut's-pennies
If bread is not properly kneaded, there is often what we call *slut's-pennies*.
—William Ellis's *Country Housewife's Family Companion*, 1780

snarley-yow
A discontented, litigious grumbler.
—Admiral William Smyth's *Sailor's Word-book*, 1867

snurpe
To become shrivelled; from Swedish *snörpa*.
—Herbert Coleridge's *Dictionary of the First, or Oldest Words in the English Language*, 1863

The Best of Forgotten English

spleenless
Kind; gentle; mild.
—John Walker's *Dictionary of the English Language*, 1835

spizzerinctum
Hard money. A fanciful coinage, as if from Latin *specie rectum*, the right kind.
—Mitford Mathews's *Dictionary of Americanisms*, 1956

spoffle
To be over busy about little or nothing. Norfolk.
—William Holloway's *Dictionary of Provincialisms*, 1838

stirrup cup
A "parting cup" given in the Highlands to guests on leaving when their feet are in the stirrups. In the north of the Highlands, called "cup at the door."
—Ebenezer Brewer's *Dictionary of Phrase and Fable*, 1898

swingebuckler
A bully who pretends to feats of arms [weaponry].
—Richard Coxe's *Pronouncing Dictionary*, 1813

T

tetricitie
The sourenesse of the countenance.
—Henry Cockeram's *Interpreter of Hard English Words*, 1623

thought-swift-flying
Flying quick as thought.
—T. Lewis Davies's *Supplementary English Glossary*, 1881

thropple
To strangle; also the wind-pipe.
—Elisha Coles's *An English Dictionary*, 1713

thwittle
A knife. "A Sheffield *thwittle* bare he." Chaucer's *Reeve's Tale*.
—William Toone's *A Glossary and Etymological Dictionary of Obsolete and Uncommon Words*, 1832

tongue-valiant
Brave in words, not in action.
—Robert Hunter's *Encyclopædic Dictionary*, 1894

touch ivory
To play at dice or billiards.
—Albert Hyamson's *Dictionary of English Phrases*, 1922

transexion
A turning from one sex to another.
—Elisha Coles's *An English Dictionary*, 1713

trilapse
A third fall into sin.
—Joseph Shipley's *Dictionary of Early English*, 1955

truttaceous
Pertaining to the trout.
—John Ogilvie's *Comprehensive English Dictionary*, 1865

tuz
A lock or tuft of hair. Not in use.
—Thomas Sheridan's *Complete Dictionary of the English Language*, 1790

U

unbuxom
Disobedient.
—Robert Hunter's *Encyclopædic Dictionary*, 1894

unlycanthropize
To change a man who had been turned into a wolf [and] back into a man again.
—T. Lewis Davies's *Supplementary English Glossary*, 1881

unseminar'd
Deprived of virility.
—Rev. Alexander Dyce's *Glossary to the Works of Shakespeare*, 1902

upright grand
Standing coition.
—Sydney Baker's *Popular Dictionary of Australian Slang*, 1943

urinarium
In agriculture, a reservoir or place for the reception of urine.
—Noah Webster's *American Dictionary of the English Language*, 1828

uveal
Belonging to a grape; like a grape.
—Edward Phillips's *New World of English Words*, 1658

uzzard
The letter z.
—James Halliwell's *Dictionary of Archaic and Provincial Words*, 1855

V

vaniloquence
Vain babbling.
—Thomas Blount's *Glossographia*, 1656

vert
To go to harbour among fern; said of a buck.
—Herbert Coleridge's *Dictionary of the First, or Oldest Words in the English Language*, 1863

versimilitude
Probability.
—William Grimshaw's *Ladies' Lexicon and Parlour Companion*, 1854

vincible
That [which] may be overcome.
—John Kersey's *New English Dictionary*, 1772

vinomadefied
Soaked with wine; formed on Latin *madefieri*, to be soaked.
—Sir James Murray's *New English Dictionary*, 1928

vitulation
A rejoicing, like a calf.
—Henry Cockeram's *Interpreter of Hard English Words*, 1623

vivarium
A place artificially prepared in which animals are kept alive, in as nearly as possible their natural state, as a park or the like; from Latin *vivus*, alive.
—Edward Lloyd's *Encyclopædic Dictionary*, 1895

voluptuary
A man given up to luxury.
—Hezekiah Burhans's *Nomenclature and Expositor*, 1833

W

Walker's bus
To go by Walker's omnibus, or *Walker's 'bus*, to walk.
—Eliezer Edwards's *Words, Facts, and Phrases*, 1882

wamblecropped
Humiliated.
—Gilbert Tucker's *American English*, 1921

wandoughty
Impotent.
—Charles Mackay's *Lost Beauties of the English Language*, 1874

wapping
Being connected with a woman.
—Rev. Thomas Fosbroke's *Encyclopædia of Antiquities*, 1843

warpiss
To cast off, put aside; adaptation of Old French *werpiss*, to quit, abandon.
—Sir James Murray's *New English Dictionary*, 1928

wheyey
Belonging to or partaking of the nature of *whey*.
—John Kersey's *New English Dictionary*, 1772

whirligigs
Testicles.
—B. E. Gent's *Dictionary of the Termes of the Canting Crew*, c. 1699

wood butcher
A carpenter; usually applied as a term of derision.
—Godfrey Irwin's *American Tramp and Underworld Slang*, 1931

woodchoir
Birds singing in a wood.
—Rev. John Boag's *Imperial Lexicon of the English Language*, c. 1850

wooden swearing
Showing anger by acts of violence, as knocking furniture about.
—J. C. Ruppenthal's *Word-List from Kansas*, 1916

wood-wool
Cotton. Fine shavings of wood used as a surgical dressing.
—Sir James Murray's *New English Dictionary*, 1928

writative
A word of [Alexander] Pope's coining, not to be imitated. "Increase of years makes men more talkative but less *writative*."
—Samuel Johnson's *Dictionary of the English Language*, 1755

wuggle
A bog or marsh.
—John Jamieson's *Etymological Dictionary of the Scottish Language*, 1808

X

xerophagy
The eating of dry meats, as a sort of fast among the primitive Christians.
—John Walker's *Dictionary of the English Language*, 1835

Y

yeoman of the mouth
An officer belonging to his Majesty's pantry.
—B.E. Gent's *Dictionary of the Termes of the Canting Crew*, 1699

Yorkshire compliment
A gift useless to the giver and not wanted by the receiver.
—Eric Partridge's *Dictionary of Slang and Unconventional English*, 1956

yowtling
An infant in arms; *yowtlings*, small things.
—Michael Traynor's *The English Dialect of Donegal*, 1953

yule-hole
The last hole to which a man could stretch his belt at a Christmas feast.
—Alexander Warrack's *Scots Dialect Dictionary*, 1911

Z

zafty
A person very easily imposed upon.
—Maj. Barzillai Lowsley's *Glossary of Berkshire Words and Phrases*, 1888

zoanthropy
A form of insanity in which a person believes himself one of the lower animals.
—William Whitney's *Century Dictionary*, 1889

zouch
An ungenteel man; a bookseller.
—John Awdeley's *Fraternitye of Vagabondes*, 1575

zowerswopped
Ill-natured.
—Thomas Wright's *Dictionary of Obsolete and Provincial English*, 1857

zythogala
In medicine, a word used frequently to signify a mixture of beer and milk.
—Daniel Fenning's *Royal English Dictionary*, 1775

The Best of Forgotten English